Proof of Performance Portfolio

Rick Nelles

Impact Publications
Manassas Park, VA

Liability/Warranty: The author and publisher have made every attempt to provide the reader with accurate information. However, they make no claims that this information will remain accurate at the time of reading. Furthermore, this information is presented for information purposes only. The author and publisher shall not be liable for any loss or damages incurred in the process of following the advice presented in this book.

Library of Congress Cataloging-in-Publication Data

Nelles, Rick
  Proof of Performance Portfolio / Rick Nelles.
    p. cm.
  Includes bibliographical references and index.
  ISBN 1-57023-148-6
  1. Employment portfolios.   2. Job Hunting   I.Title.

HF5383 .N38 2000
650.14—dc21

00-061373

Publisher: For information, including current and forthcoming publications, authors, press kits, and submission guidelines, visit: *www.impactpublications.com*

Publicity/Rights: For information on publicity, author interviews, and subsidiary rights, contact Media Relations: Tel. 703-361-7300 or Fax 703-335-9486.

Sales/Distribution: For information on distribution or quantity discount rates, call (703-361-7300), fax (703-335-9486), e-mail (*questions@impactpublications.com*) or write: Sales Department, Impact Publications, 9104 Manassas Drive, Suite N, Manassas Park, VA 20111. Bookstore orders should be directed to our trade distributor: National Book Network, 15200 NBN Way, Blue Ridge Summit, PA 17214, Tel. 1-800-462-6420.

Layout and Design by C. M. Chapman

Contents

IN DEDICATION

To Maxine Nelles, my mother, who never gave up on my dream and who helped finance the start of this project in my life.

Thanks Mom!

ACKNOWLEDGMENTS

For over twenty years, I have recruited for and worked with hundreds of hiring managers, both in small and large companies. In order to fill their need for the best people for the job, I had to interview thousands of candidates. Most of the information in this book came from observing and working with these hiring managers and the candidates. I want to extend my gratitude to all of them, for without them this book would never have come to be.

I also want to thank Mike Weddle and Mark Bradley for their editing help. They made the book easy to read, fun, and to the point. The enthusiasm of my agent, Dan Verdick, has helped make this book a career dream come true for me.

Finally, I want to thank everyone at Impact Publications for their hard work and dedication to helping people with career development, and for believing in the Proof of Performance!

Rick Nelles

Preface

I remember graduating from college and how lost and uncomfortable I felt in looking for that first full-time professional job, a job that I hoped would kick-start my career. Coming from the small town of Elk River, Minnesota, I was naïve to the ways of the big city and of big business. If an interviewer would have said, "Boo!," I probably would have tipped over in my chair! It was a fearful and stressful time for me. Now, after 20 years as a professional recruiter (some call us "head-hunters"), I look back at that time and realize that it didn't have to be that way at all.

You see, I'd made several crucial mistakes:

- I waited until my last quarter of college to prepare for my job search.

- I didn't take advantage of the college placement center's services. (What was I thinking? It was free!)

- I hadn't saved or asked for any documents that would prove my performance.

- I 'winged it' going into interviews, thinking they would hire me on my good looks and great personality.

- I had no written career goals, and didn't even really know what I wanted to do.

I could go on, but you get the point. I thought a great job would *find me*. After all, I was a college graduate, and I communicated well with people. I'd paid my dues, and now the business world *owed* me a good job!

Why didn't some professor pull me aside, shake me hard, and tell me that you can't just "wing it" in a job search or interview? Why didn't my parents educate me to this fact? I guess it all boils down to **my failing to take responsibility for my career direction.**

I founded Career Directions, Inc. with this mission:

We help direct people to the right information that will empower and inspire them to reach their professional career dreams.

We want to help people take responsibility for their careers. The information you are about to read in the *Proof of Performance Portfolio* is the result of over 20 years of observing people win the best job offers. We have placed over 800 people in jobs and, for each job offer, we've had to interview an average of 20 to 30 candidates. We'll share the techniques and true stories of what your best competition is doing to get the job *you* may want and deserve.

Career Directions, Inc. places people in sales positions, so our stories are concentrated in that area. However, the techniques we teach can be applied to any profession and in any organization, private or public. Never forget—regardless of what type of job you are pursuing—you must market and sell yourself. Every time you interview for a job, you are the sales person and the product!

Don't be like I was when I graduated—totally unprepared and scared to death! People who learn the game of career transition and play it well have much less fear, anxiety, and doubt in their job quests. By reading this book, you've taken a significant, proactive step in your career. We salute you for this!

- Rick Nelles, President, Career Directions, Inc.

Part I

Laying the Groundwork

❖ Why You Need a Portfolio

❖ A Winning Attitude

1

Why You Need a
Proof of Performance Portfolio

I t was just another day of interviewing candidates. After 20 years of recruiting and interviewing, I'd heard it all. This particular candidate (we'll call him Bill) was telling me the same old story I'd heard a thousand times before. He was listing great accomplishment after great accomplishment and bragging about what a great salesperson he was.

On this day, though, my skepticism increased as Bill went on and on in a fashion reminiscent of Jon Lovitz doing his old Saturday Night Live liar routine — "Yeah...and then I was named, uhhh .... Salesman of the Year — yeah, that's the ticket!" As Bill rambled on, my mind then flipped to another famous scene, this one from the movie Jerry Maguire. I thought of the scene where Maguire was trying to get Rod Tidwell to remain his client. As Maguire gave reason after reason, Tidwell made one bottom-line request, "SHOW ME THE MONEY!" As I recalled the shot of Tidwell dancing around in his towel, shouting "Show me the money," a smile came across my face. In my mind, I began to dance around shouting, **"SHOW ME THE PROOF!"**

That was it! I shouldn't have to sit there and try to guess which of Bill's stories were true and which were pure B.S.! Candidates should be able to show me some PROOF of what they claimed! Bill saw my smile turn into a devilish grin. Before he could launch into his next self-aggrandizing litany, I jumped in and nearly shouted, **"SHOW ME THE PROOF!"** Bill immediately took on the 'deer-in-the-headlights' look. Stunned, he stammered, "Uh...well...I don't have any actual proof." His lame explanations of why he had no proof had all the validity of the old 'dog ate my homework' excuse.

Bill left the office, realizing his bluff had been called, and I sat back in my chair with a great sense of relief that I had not subjected my client to this impostor and liar. What if that guy had been hired? It would have only been a matter of months before it became obvious that he couldn't perform. It would have cost my client thousands of dollars, and it would have cost me a good client! It was obvious that I would have to ask all candidates to "show me the proof" in the future.

Thinking back over my two decades of recruiting, I remembered that the best candidates had used career portfolios to document their successes. So I started teaching candidates how to gather documentation to prove their claims. I began to see amazing results. Candidates developed much greater confidence going into interviews, and hiring managers raved about the candidates I sent them! The performance portfolio worked.

From that modest, almost accidental, beginning, the portfolio idea has grown into the complete **Proof of Performance Portfolio** system. The information you now hold in your hand will ensure that you'll find your ideal career. You will have the documentation, the confidence, and the interviewing skills to get the job!

What Your Best Competition is Doing to Get the Job You Want

Successful people all know one thing— **to get the best jobs, you must be ready to compete at the highest level.** It doesn't matter whether jobs in general are abundant or scarce, there is always enormous competition for the most lucrative and satisfying employment. If you want one of those jobs, you must be able to stand above your fellow candidates.

Professional sports teams get to see their competition in action. Coaches and scouts watch films to help prepare their team for future opponents. You don't have that advantage. You never see the other candidates interviewing. The material in this book will help you solve that problem! We've scouted your best competition! We've recruited them, we've interviewed them and, in this book, we will show you some of the tools they're using to land the best jobs available.

The major theme of this book is that **the best job candidates always back up everything they claim on their résumé with documentation that proves it.** Our research indicates that this strategy alone can increase a job candidate's success rate by more than 400 percent! That's because employers are looking to hire people who can produce results, and a documented past history is the best guarantee an employer can get that a candidate will produce those results.

Hiring managers are under a great deal of pressure to find the right candidate for the position they're seeking to fill. Most managers can't afford to make a bad hire. When a candidate doesn't work out, it costs the company thousands of dollars in wages, training, and lost production, not to mention the expense of launching a new search for someone to fill the position. That's why hiring managers are elated when candidates back up their résumés with documented proof that they are professionally who they say they are! Proof of performance candidates make the hiring manager's job easier. They can be much more confident that the new employee will be able to perform.

Why Employers Will Appreciate Your Documentation

"A few highly publicized employer-defamation verdicts have changed what information employers give about their own employees and how they get facts on job applications . . . . Companies give out only limited information such as dates of employment, because they are scared of being sued," says Michael R. Losey, president of the Society for Human Resource Management . . . .

"In an Equifax, Inc. survey, 77% of companies said they couldn't make sound business decisions about applicants because previous employers wouldn't provide the necessary background data, even though, as Losey notes, 'references are more reliable than resumes or interviews for predicting' job performance . . . ."

> "Cautiously worded references devoid of personal and performance information create more problems than they solve."
> - USA Today

"Show Me the Proof!"

Hiring managers receive many great looking résumés, filled with lists of impressive accomplishments. The manager's goal is to determine if the contents of the résumés are true. There are three primary problems that are driving hiring managers to shout, "Show me the proof!"

❖ Recently, companies have discontinued giving references of former employees. The only information available are dates of employment. They give no other information, and hiring managers are seldom able to get proof of performance from a former employer.

❖ Unscrupulous interviewees realize that it's impossible to check their claims, and they have become very bold about stretching facts during interviews and falsifying their résumés. Hiring managers who have been stung by dishonest job candidates have become very skeptical. They would love to see proof of these performance claims.

❖ The final frustration for hiring managers is the inability to get reliable references. If the candidate has given a name as a reference, it's very unlikely that the reference will be negative. How is the hiring manager to know whether the person giving the recommendation is reliable? Hiring managers almost need references on the people giving references!

**If You Have No Documentation, This is
What Companies May Have to DO**

"Some companies screen job candidates by searching government databases of criminal activities. Others use industrial psychologists or bring in temporary employees and only offer permanent jobs after they have proved themselves. And, says *The Seattle Times*, some even resort to handwriting experts such as Hannah McFarland to help determine who is right for a job or promotion. Giving new meaning to the word 'loophole,' McFarland advises that people who leave o's and a's open at the bottom can't be trusted with money."

- USA Today

The **Proof of Performance (PoP) Portfolio** is designed to solve all these problems. Using this book, you'll develop powerful documentation of your accomplishments. The **PoP Portfolio** will become your best interviewing tool, documenting and offering professional proof that you can do the job. It will help you organize documentation of your accomplishments, provide evidence of your skills and highlight your strengths. It will minimize concerns about your weaknesses. The **PoP Portfolio** will give you a definitive competitive edge over everyone else in the job market, by providing evidence that you are a person who rewards an employer with results!

Interviewing With Impact

All résumés begin to look alike to a busy hiring manager, especially during interviews. Your portfolio creates a unique and memorable impression for the hiring manager. Long after the interviews are over, you'll be the candidate they can't forget! Educators have found that people only remember about 5 percent of what they hear, but **when people are able to hear something and also see it in a visual format, their retention rates increase dramatically.** When you use a colorful portfolio filled with graphs, pictures, certificates, stories, and awards that document your past successes and back up your words, you're communicating with great impact. Your portfolio stamps an indelible impression on the interviewer's mind. It also validates the truthfulness of your claims. When you leave the room, the interviewer doesn't need to determine whether you are a person who can perform. You've removed any doubt by providing documentation to support your claims. **All else being equal, a person with only a résumé will lose a job offer to a candidate with a professional portfolio that backs up his/her résumé.**

> "It's the start that stops most people."
>
> *- Bits & Pieces* magazine

Portfolios vs. Résumés

The purpose of the résumé is to provide the hiring manager enough reason to talk to you about an opportunity. **The résumé is not meant to be a tool to help you in the interview.** In the interview, your job is to support what's on the résumé and prove to the hiring manager that you are a person who can produce results. As we mentioned, hiring managers have learned that many résumés are embellished and that some contain outright lies. Since they can't check out every claim, many hiring managers have become skeptical of every résumé. Unfortunately, many job seekers count on their résumé to "sell" them to the hiring manager. **The purpose of your portfolio is to document and support the claims on your résumé and assure the hiring manager that you are the person you say you are and your résumé claims you are.** That's how you sell yourself in an interview!

Why Doesn't Everyone Have a Proof Of Performance Portfolio?

Portfolios are not commonly used because most people still operate on the false assumption that a résumé is the only job-seeking document they need. There are three underlying causes of this belief:

❖ **Most people have never thought of building a portfolio.** They have no idea that they can use documents and other proofs of performance to build a powerful portfolio that will shed light on their skills, abilities, and accomplishments. The best candidates *have* discovered this tool, but haven't shared it with others. They don't want to lose their competitive advantage!

❖ **It's difficult to find information on developing a professional career portfolio.** Very little has been written on this subject. On rare occasions, a book on job seeking will mention a portfolio, but no one has given it comprehensive treatment — until now!

❖ Even if they've thought about it or read about it, **most job candidates never use a proof of performance strategy because they just don't want to take the time to do it.** They don't want to gather documents. They don't want to objectively analyze their strengths and weaknesses. They don't want to ask employers or teachers for referral letters. They don't want to dig through files for credentials or other papers. They simply don't want to do the work.

The Time to Start is Now!

If you don't have a portfolio at this time, don't feel badly. You're not alone! The good news is that you have purchased this book and are about to embark on a great career adventure, building your own **PoP Portfolio!** This is leading-edge career-transition information and with it you'll learn how to create a tool that you'll use to get the job you really want.

Do you have misgivings about the need for this process? You might think that your good grades, well-written résumé, and strong references will be enough to land your dream job. **You may believe that your track record speaks for itself. You're wrong!** Your 'track record' is simply a list of things you have allegedly done. You need to provide documentation that will give substance to your track record and bring it alive for the interviewer!

You might also feel a little overwhelmed by the thought of going to the trouble of building a portfolio. But consider this: which of these tasks would you deem to be more important—landing a great job in your chosen career or successfully completing a term paper? We hope that you'd say that a satisfying career or job is one of the most important things you can pursue in life. Yet many people would spend more time preparing a term paper than preparing for a career transition! People spend thousands of hours and tens of thousands of dollars on formal education, but fail to spend any time preparing for the transition to get the job they want. As you will see, it's often just a small extra investment of time that separates those who get the best jobs from those who must settle for mediocrity.

Fortunately, **this book gives you a systematic approach to the process.** We'll give you step-by-step instructions for assembling your documents and developing outstanding interviewing skills. While it may take some time and effort initially to develop your portfolio, we can assure you that the results will be worth the effort! The more time you invest in your portfolio, the more valuable it will become. After you start your portfolio, it will become easier and even fun to update. By starting your portfolio **now**, you'll have a clear advantage over the majority of your competition for the rest of your life.

And there **will** be competition! Like it or not, the market for the best jobs is extremely competitive. **If you're unwilling to put some effort into your job campaign, you'll be frustrated much of your life,** as you watch less talented people win the jobs you want. It may not seem fair, but if you don't learn how to promote yourself in the job market and set yourself apart from your competition, you'll never achieve your full earning potential. You'll never have the satisfaction of knowing you are using your skills to reach your best level of job accomplishment.

The fact that you're reading this is a great start! **The information in this book wasn't developed in an 'ivory tower.'** It's the result of our personal observations and study of how people separate themselves from their competition in career transition. We'll share some true stories of how people overcame their fears and took positive steps to get their dream jobs. We hope these stories will provide the motivational fuel that will drive you to build an outstanding portfolio and sharpen your career transition skills!

"If no one ever took risks, Michaelangelo would have painted the Sistine floor."

- Neil Simon

Using This Book

Notice that we have left wide margins in which you can write notes. As you read this book, you'll have many ideas for documentation pieces that you can gather for yourself. **Make note of those ideas in the margins as they occur to you!** If you don't write them down as you think of them, you might forget some great ideas for documentation.

A second important thing you should do is **make several copies of all the forms in the Master Forms section in the back of this book.** Don't write on the Master Forms themselves! You'll need lots of copies of those forms to help you plan and build your portfolio.

The third thing you will want to do is **purchase a package of plastic or vinyl sheet protectors** from your local office supply store. We suggest buying at least 25 to begin. All pieces of your documentation will be kept in sheet protectors, so they can be placed in your binder as a part of your **Proof of Performance Portfolio** package. The binder will become the place where you'll keep and carry all the important proofs of performance that you gather. By keeping all this information in your portfolio, you'll be able to find it easily each time you begin a new phase of career transition.

Continuing Career Growth

The initial reason you purchased this book may have been to get a new job, but your **Proof of Performance Portfolio** can also be used to enhance and speed up your career advancement within your current company. By gathering documentation of your on-going successes, you'll be able to use your portfolio to demonstrate to your managers and supervisors that you're striving to be the best in your current position. This book will teach you how to document your current successes constantly and creatively!

The time to start gathering documentation is NOW, not when you get fired or laid off. You should be gathering documentation as you succeed. This has become more important today than ever, since many companies no longer give out references of any kind.

This leaves many people with no documentation of performance from an outside source. You must learn to gather and develop these documents yourself, while you're in your current job. To our knowledge, this is the only book that teaches you this technique.

What if I Don't Have Anything to Document?

For some people, this book may be a real wake-up call! As you begin to build your **PoP Portfolio,** you may realize that you don't have a lot of accomplishments. You may have been just putting in time at your job and not striving for excellence. If, after working through this book, you realize that you don't have many accomplishments from your past work experience, don't be discouraged. You can begin to change that right now! Seek out opportunities in which you can get results that make a difference, then use your **PoP Portfolio** materials to document your successes. You'll find that your job satisfaction and self-esteem will greatly increase as you do this. It will be your first step toward real success in your career!

Other Tools in the Proof of Performance Portfolio

The **Proof of Performance Portfolio** is made up of many other tools that will contribute to the development of your own personal portfolio and the growth of your career.

❖ The **Expanding Your Career Transition Comfort Zone Worksheet** *(Form 1)* will help you visually track your progress in building your own personal job-seeking skills.

❖ Our **Proactive Documentation Planner** *(Form 2)* will help you lay out a step-by-step game plan with detailed descriptions, dates, and goals to gather the right kind of documents to prove you are a top performer.

❖ You can use the **Network Planning Worksheet** *(Form 5)* to effectively network with people who can help you grow your career. You'll find several other helpful tools as you work through each module in this book.

Growing Through Career Transition

If you're beginning to feel a little anxiety as you contemplate your career transition – or perhaps a lot of anxiety, be assured that it's perfectly normal and that you're not alone. For most people, looking for a job is one of the most stressful times in their lives. If you're involuntarily out of work, the stress is even more intense. **However, it is possible to turn this anxiety around and even have some fun during this period of your life!** And we're not talking only about the kind of fun that allows you temporarily to forget your situation. That sort of escapism is fine, but **the real key to being effective in your job search is to enjoy the process!** This will be a journey of self-discovery and personal fulfillment, as well as a technique for finding good employment.

Learning about yourself as you assemble a powerful career-transition tool will help you eliminate fear and anxiety better than anything else we know of. We've been amazed at how people completely change their attitudes about finding a job once they've learned about our **PoP Portfolio** process. Your career transition project can turn an ordinary job search into a unique adventure that is the very essence of life, GROWTH!

2

Developing a Winning Attitude

everal years ago, tennis professional Andre Agassi teamed up with Canon U.S.A., Inc. to promote their cameras. The promotion stated "Image is everything," capitalizing on the rebel image of Agassi. With apologies to Mr. Agassi and Canon, we believe "attitude is everything" in becoming successful. Image is merely a superficial surface thing—attitude is at the core of who we are.

> "Your living is determined not so much by what life brings to you as by the attitude you bring to life; not so much by what happens to you as by the way your mind looks at what happens."
> - John Homer Miller

In the chapters that follow, we'll give you specific instructions on how to assemble a **Proof of Performance Portfolio** that will be a powerful tool in your career search. We'll also help you to develop techniques for effective networking, researching, and interviewing, which will make sure that you'll find just the right career and job. But the most important starting point is to develop a positive, winning attitude!

A good attitude is absolutely essential to your success in seeking a new job. We're confident that the techniques you'll learn in this book will make your career transition an interesting, exciting, and enjoyable process, but there will also be times when you'll feel overwhelmed, tired, and a little discouraged. At those times, it's vital that you keep a winning attitude! Many times, your attitude will be the only thing that sets you apart from your competition.

Therefore, in this chapter, we'll focus on seven basic aspects of a winning attitude:

❖ **Overcoming Fear**

❖ **Expanding Your Career Transition Comfort Zone**

❖ **Persistence**

❖ **Enthusiasm**

❖ **Commitment to Excellence**

❖**Competitive Spirit**

❖ **Supportive Lifestyle**

Before we proceed, we should address a question you might be asking right now: "Do I have to try to become someone I'm not in order to succeed in my career search? Do I have to act like a fast-talking TV huckster or a glad-handing used-car salesman to be successful?" ABSOLUTELY NOT! **The goal of this chapter, and of this entire book, is to present YOU in the best possible light!** If you're a basically quiet person, you don't have to become a "life-of-the-party" type to get a job. After all, your ultimate goal should be to find a job that is so fulfilling that you can't wait to get up each day and go to work. And that job will suit your personality as well as your qualifications. So, at no time do we advise you to 'fake it' in order to get hired. It's dishonest and you'd never be able to 'fake it' on the job over the long haul. **Who you are is unique and precious. You have the ability to make an outstanding contribution to your chosen field.** Our goal is to help you believe that and to project it to others. So let's get at it!

Overcoming Fear

Even during periods of very low unemployment, there are still large numbers of people who do not achieve their career goals. Examples include college graduates who settle for jobs that are less satisfying and rewarding than they had hoped for; mid-life professionals whose careers have stagnated; and underemployed people in every walk of life who are not reaching their full career potential. While these people can often cite numerous external reasons for their predicament, the majority of them are in this situation because of an internal issue, FEAR. Fear is the number one enemy of people in career transition. We have seen well-qualified candidates falter in their career transition because they couldn't overcome their fear of some of the basic tasks in a job search. Sadly, they failed to get a job which could give them the financial rewards and job satisfaction they desired and deserved.

The Fear of Getting Started

One of the biggest challenges in career transition is simply 'getting off the dime.' This may come from a fear that the process seems so big, so daunting, that just the thought of it is paralyzing. The **Proof of Performance Portfolio** is designed to help overcome this fear by breaking down the project into manageable tasks. You'll find that you can **start by doing things that are simple and non-threatening** and soon you'll actually be enjoying the process. We'll deal with this in more detail in the next section, "Expanding Your Career Transition Comfort Zone."

"People-Phobia"

Many job-seekers have a basic fear of meeting and talking with others. This is a serious problem, because most of what you'll be doing in your career search involves dealing with people, many of them new to you. Almost all the activities we discuss in Part III, "Your Job Search Campaign," involve 'people skills.' So, even if the career you ultimately seek involves dealing with information or things rather than with people, you will need to be comfortable dealing with people in order to get that job! The best way to overcome "people-phobia" is to **take small steps, becoming comfort-**

able with friends-of-friends and others with whom you have much in common. Eventually, you'll be able to cold-call complete strangers with confidence and ease. The step-by-step approach outlined in "Expanding Your Career Transition Comfort Zone" should be helpful to you with this fear, as well.

The Fear of Asking for Help and Advice

One of the most important things you can do during your career transition is to ask for help. You'll need help from others in order to assemble your portfolio successfully, to expand your network, and to get informational interviews. Asking for help is so important that we can say flat out that **those who do not learn the art of asking for help and advice during career transition WILL FAIL and fall short of their expectations to get the job they really want.** People are your greatest resource in career transition, but you must ask them in order to receive the help you need! Fortunately, there are two important points that can reduce your discomfort in asking for advice.

> "Do the thing you fear and keep on doing it . . . that is the quickest and surest way ever yet discovered to conquer fear."
>
> *- Dale Carnegie*

First of all, **there is absolutely no shame in asking others for help!** Every successful person had help from others along the way—

career advice, professional mentoring, business referrals, financial assistance, etc. The myth of the totally self-made person is just that, a myth, and anyone who claims to have achieved success without any help is being dishonest.

Second, you should realize that **most people are complimented when you ask them for help or advice!** The fact that you're consulting them is a sign of your respect and admiration for them. Successful people also realize that they have a responsibility to help others as their mentors once helped them. When you ask for help, they will see this as an opportunity to give back something of what they once received.

There will be times when someone refuses to help you. Please realize that this person is in the minority. Learning the art of asking includes learning to deal with being turned down occasionally, but you should understand that the **success is in overcoming the fear of asking!** When turned down, simply say out loud, "I'm glad I tried and, even though my attempt didn't work this time, I feel good because I'm taking the right actions to get the job I want."

Additional Help

If you still have difficulty asking for help, we suggest that you read *The Aladdin Factor* by Jack Canfield and Mark Victor Hansen. This book will teach you how to ask for help in many situations and overcome the fear of doing so. It will teach many other lessons that will help you in your professional career and personal life as well.

"Stage Fright"

When you get to the formal interview stage, you may feel the same kind of fear that performers and public speakers feel—the fear of being in the spotlight, the fear of being judged in public. One professional actor we know says that he overcame his stage fright once he realized that the audience, by spending money for tickets, had a financial investment in his being good. He realized that the audience wanted him to be good, that they were on his side!

Much the same can be said for your job interview. The company is on your side. They've made a financial investment in your being the right candidate. They may have made a substantial investment, if they've covered your expenses for travel, lodging, etc., to interview for the position. A hiring manager is especially anxious that you do well. It's the manager's job to find and hire the best candidates, so that manager has a definite stake in your being the right person. If you look good, the manager looks good. The manager is on your side. Some hiring managers, even seasoned professional interviewers, say that they're more nervous than the candidate in an interview! You should also know that, as someone they've invited in for an interview, you're as good as any other candidate they'll see and you absolutely deserve to be there!

Fear of Rejection

This is probably the most basic fear of all in the job search process. "What if I do all this work, all this research, all this preparation, and I don't get the job?" First of all, you have to accept that some rejection is part of the process. Unless you land the perfect job at your first interview, you're bound to have some rejections before you find the job you want. Successful people see rejection not as a step backward, but as a step forward, getting closer to success. A job search has been described as "No, No, No, No, No, No, Yes," so a "No" is bringing you closer to that ultimate "Yes!"

You can also allay your fear of rejection by knowing that, in an interview, you're interviewing them as much as they're interviewing you! That is, there are things you can learn about a company only in your interview. Your research and informational interviewing will have told you that you would probably like that company, but you won't know for sure until you're actually there, meeting your prospective supervisors and co-workers. If your interviewer seems intent on making you uncomfortable, perhaps asking trick questions, etc., this may be a major clue that you wouldn't want to work for that company. You have the right to say "No" as much as they do!

For each section of this chapter, we'll give you an affirmation, a positive statement that you can use to reinforce your growth in that area. Say the statement out loud, as often as you like.

Affirmation for Overcoming Fear:

To deal with your fear, repeat the following: **"I do not let fear stand in the way of getting a great job. I feel the fear and do it anyway!"**

> "Comfort zones are plush-lined coffins. When you stay in your plush-lined coffin, you die."
>
> *- Stan Dale*

Expanding Your Career Transition Comfort Zone

Closely related to overcoming fear is the concept of expanding your 'Career Transition Comfort Zone.' We all prefer to engage in those activities we find enjoyable, fulfilling, and familiar. Conversely, we tend to avoid activities that are unfamiliar, because we feel uncomfortable in those situations. In short, we tend to stay in our Comfort Zone. This is a normal reaction that often helps to keep us safe and secure by avoiding foolish risks. But **staying in our Career Transition Comfort Zone can keep us from growing, learning, and achieving our full potential!**

This is why many job hunters never reach their full career potential. Looking to stay within their Career Transition Comfort Zone, they do what most other job hunters do: they respond to want ads, mail résumés blindly, and depend upon "fate" to help them find that perfect job. They keep their goals modest to minimize the chance of failure. The only thing that ever forces them out of their Comfort Zone is desperation!

While there are many people who fail to expand their Comfort Zone, **there is another group of people who leap far from** their Comfort Zone without proper preparation. We might admire their adventurous spirit but, much of the time, they're destined to fail. Job-seekers of this type might go right into a formal interview without preparation. That's like taking up tennis one day and trying to play Wimbledon the next. Disaster and humiliation are assured! Others of this type might do something outrageous, such as standing outside company headquarters with a bullhorn or calling the CEO at home to ask for a job. You occasionally hear of a stunt like this being effective but, in general, these kinds of shenanigans are seen as grossly unprofessional.

Successful people, on the other hand, don't take outlandish risks outside their Comfort Zone, nor do they stay within its cozy and stifling cocoon. Instead, **successful people work systematically to EXPAND their Comfort Zone!** They identify an area in which they need to feel more comfortable and then take well-planned steps to become more at ease in that situation. They know that they'll make some mistakes and that they'll face the occasional rejection, but they persevere, taking these calculated risks. Soon, they're completely comfortable doing something that may have terrified them only a short time before. Expanding your Comfort Zone will allow you to create more opportunities, develop new skills, expand your professional relationships, and build confidence.

How to Expand Your Comfort Zone

The best way to expand your Comfort Zone is to begin doing the actions that cause the least amount of discomfort and then work your way up to actions that are the most uncomfortable or important, such as the formal interview. Make several copies of the **Expanding Your Comfort Zone Worksheet** (*Form 2*). At the top, identify the area you'd like to work on. For example, let's say you're uncomfortable making phone calls to people you don't know. Sales people call this "cold calling," and you'll be doing a lot of it in your job-seeking campaign!

Cold Calling Gives Rewards

As a young salesperson, I was scared to death to do cold calling and was struggling in my new sales position. Fortunately, I had a great sales manager who suggested that I set a goal and then reward myself when I accomplished that goal.

I love to play great golf courses, so I set a goal of 10 cold calls. My reward would be to play the beautiful Interlachen Country Club once I completed that goal.

I was able to complete my cold calls in two days. I loved playing that course but, more importantly, I found out that cold calling and introducing myself to strangers was something I could do, and do well. Like any other skill, it was a little scary at first, but there are incredible benefits from learning to do it!

- Rick Nelles

At the top of your worksheet, write "Cold Calling." Then write down some calls you need to make that are unlikely to cause you much anxiety. Perhaps you need to call your college registrar to request a copy of your transcript. Note when you completed the call successfully. Then you might need to call a former employer to ask for a recommendation. Make the call and record the date. Next, you might call someone who works in the career you're pursuing, but who is unlikely to have any "power" over you. Again, note the date you made the successful call. With each step, you're expanding your Comfort Zone, so that before long, you can call new people and request information and advice with complete confidence and assurance.

Of course, this exercise will be different for everyone. There will be some people who love cold calling, but can't stand gathering reference letters and documentation. As you read through this book, make marginal notes on which activities will be easy and which will be uncomfortable for you. But in all cases we do advise using the Worksheets. By providing a record of your progress, they'll help you in two important ways. First, they'll give you a definite sense of accomplishment as you proceed. This ongoing reward will give you increased confidence and faster progress. Second, your worksheets will give you documentation of a successful personal growth project, which you can show to the hiring manager in an interview.

Affirmation for Expanding Comfort Zones:

"I work every day to expand my comfort zone by trying new activities in small, manageable steps."

Persistence

We believe that the **Proof of Performance Portfolio** is the best tool you can ever have to ensure a successful career transition. Many people, however, will read this book, get excited, get started on a portfolio, and then fail to follow through. You must dedicate yourself to doing what this book tells you to do. **The instructions given in this book are not shortcuts to a better career. There are no shortcuts — it takes hard work.** You need not only to read this book, but to **do** the things we teach you! Doing only parts of the book will not give you the power you need to get the very best jobs. Persist in your job search, and make the effort to do the required work thoroughly. You should realize that employers are looking for people who can dedicate themselves to a task and go all out. The completion of your **PoP Portfolio** will show employers that you're dedicated to success and that you'll persist in achieving your goals.

One way you can help yourself to persist in your efforts is to set short-term goals and then reward yourself. In our cold-calling example, you might set a goal to call 10 people to arrange for informational interviews and then plan a reward for yourself upon completion of the task.

> "Nothing in the world can take the place of persistence. Talent will not; nothing is more common than unsuccessful men with talent. Genius will not; unrewarded genius is almost a proverb. Education will not; the world is full of educated derelicts. Persistence and determination alone are omnipotent.

> The slogan 'press on' has solved and always will solve the problems of the human race."
>
> *- Calvin Coolidge*

Affirmation for Persistence:

"I persist in my career quest every day. I finish what I start, and reward myself along the way for tasks completed successfully."

Enthusiasm

One of the attitudes that can overcome many shortcomings is enthusiasm. Many hiring managers will pass over candidates who don't appear to have the enthusiasm and energy to do the job. People who don't project a sense of passion and excitement about the position can lose out, even if they have the best qualifications. Conversely, **an enthusiastic person may win a job over a lackluster person who is better qualified,** at least on paper.

Are you an enthusiastic person? Do you project that enthusiasm? How would you rank yourself on a scale of one to ten? Ask three friends how they would rank you. In your job interviewing process, you must display enthusiasm right from the first phone call. Without enthusiasm and energy in that first call, you may never get an interview! (*In Part III, we advise practicing your phone skills with a tape recorder. One of the most important things you can do is to learn to project enthusiasm in your phone voice. Listen to your taped practice sessions. Does the person on the tape excite you? Does he project his voice with energy and confidence? If not, continue to practice until you feel excited by the enthusiasm of the person on tape.)*

We should stress again that we don't advise you to try to fake it! Nothing rings so hollow as a forced "rah-rah" kind of attitude. Unless you're a brilliant improvisational actor, artificial enthusiasm is worse than none at all. What you should do is **keep your own genuine excitement and enthusiasm going!** Do this by keeping your eyes on the ultimate prize of an exciting new career, by enjoying the career transition process and by taking pleasure in doing and learning new things and meeting new people. Let that energy carry you forward and infect all your job search activities!

Affirmation for Enthusiasm:

"I am enthusiastic, and optimistic about my job search. Others can see and admire my energy and positive outlook."

> "Nothing great was ever achieved without enthusiasm."
> *- Ralph Waldo Emerson*

Commitment to Excellence

Your current career transition could well mean a lifetime of prosperity and personal fulfillment for you and for your loved ones. This is not the time to take shortcuts or to try to get by on less than your very best! Your **Proof of Performance Portfolio** will be indicative of the effort that you plan to give to your future employer, and it will show how committed you are to doing excellent work. If your portfolio is poorly put together, it can become a liability. As you assemble your portfolio, ask yourself:

❖ Does my portfolio project a sense of competence and professionalism?

❖ Is my portfolio well organized and easy to use?

❖ Are my documents neatly displayed and easy to read?

❖ Have I used color and graphics for maximum impact?

❖ Does my portfolio show me in a complete, accurate, and positive light?

Be sure that your portfolio is a representation of your commitment to excellence. Actually, you have an advantage in this project, because it's entirely your own. Your portfolio is your professional projection of yourself, and you should do everything you can to ensure that it comes up to your vision.

Affirmation for Commitment to Excellence:

"I settle for nothing less than my very best. I am committed to excellence in all my activities and I take great pride in my work."

> "The quality of a person's life is in direct proportion to their commitment to excellence, regardless of their chosen field of endeavor."
>
> *- Vince Lombardi*

Competitive Spirit

"Competition" is almost a sacred word in America. Nearly everyone pays lip service to competition as one of our core values, but rarely does anyone say exactly what it means. Examples of competition are all around us. Nations compete economically and militarily. Corporations compete in the marketplace. Politicians compete for power and influence. Even parents must compete with the many negative influences that vie for the attention of their children. Life is all about competition. Competition is everywhere we look, but what exactly do we mean by a competitive spirit?

First of all, the kind of competition we admire is not a desire to degrade and humiliate others or to get ahead at any cost. Unfortunately, there are some people who seem to have that attitude. We can find them in all walks of life, from sports to politics to business. These people are very poor role models and, although their cutthroat tactics may gain them some measure of success, they are not to be admired or emulated. **The true competitive spirit we admire is the desire to become the best in your field of endeavor and the faith that, in being the best, you will be rewarded.**

Career Transition Lessons in
Dedication From the Golf Course

My passion for golf runs deep. In high school, I would have trouble competing in tournaments on courses with a lot of sand bunkers. One day, my coach told me that if I wanted to be good at golf, I needed to work at the weak aspects of my game.

He gave some pointers on hitting sand shots, threw me in a sand trap with a hundred balls, and said, "Don't come out until you learn how to hit a sand shot." After that, I became a very good sand player.

You should treat career transition the same way. Find out what your weaknesses are and get someone who can coach you on what you need to do to overcome those weaknesses. Finally, *you must practice.* It wasn't just my coach's pointers, but my time in the bunker that prepared me for the course. A strong competitive attitude focuses on preparation and practice.

-Rick Nelles

For some people, a competitive spirit comes easily. They've been raised since childhood with a love for competition, in sports, in academics, in the arts, whatever their particular field may be. They seem able to do what it takes to be the best, almost without effort, and they take their triumphs in stride. Other people seem less competitive. They settle for less than their best efforts and they may or may not be happy with their resulting lot in life. Still others may resist the idea of competition altogether.

Which type of person are you? It's important to develop a healthy competitive spirit in your career transition, because the job market is one of the most competitive environments you will ever encounter! **In order to succeed in career transition and to find the best job with the best pay and highest job satisfaction, you must compete.** There are only a limited number of jobs out there that are ideal for you, and many, many people want those jobs. Again, you must compete for those jobs.

Remember that the competitive spirit means that you do everything you can to be the best at what you do. Assemble the most powerful documentation you can. Find out what your best competition is doing and learn from them. Talk to hiring managers and people who have the jobs you want, and find out how they got the job. Practice diligently at your phone and interviewing skills. In short, strive to be the best in your field. When you do succeed, you can feel good that your success was well earned!

Affirmation for Competitive Spirit:

"I work hard and prepare diligently to become the best in my field. I am successful because I deserve it."

Winning By a Nose

I was recruiting for the nation's number one medical supply company, and their Sales Manager had flown in to interview four finalist candidates at the airport. These four were selected from a field of more than sixty candidates and all four were superbly qualified. The Sales Manager called me just before he boarded his plane to tell me that my candidates were among the best that he had ever interviewed. Then he said that I should have one of the candidates, her name was Bridget, call his secretary ASAP because she would be flying to Chicago for two days, *and 10 interviews!*

I was puzzled that he had picked Bridget so quickly, and I asked him what set her apart from the other excellent candidates. He said that she'd done two things during her interview that made an impression. First, halfway through the interview, she had looked squarely at him and said, "Steve, your company has a little problem in the marketplace." Then she paused. Steve said he was thinking this was a pretty gutsy thing to do in an interview, telling him that she knew they were the number one company, but that they had problems out there. He said he was anxious for her to explain.

After pausing (an effective way to get someone's full attention), she said, "Let me tell you where I got that information. You see, I called five of your biggest hospital customers and talked to the buyers. They told me that when you guys implemented your ordering process through a P.C. system, it wasn't all that user-friendly. Some of the buyers felt that your system was taking away some of their decision-making power, and that your company was trying to monopolize the system." She then went on to say, "I could see that inventory would be better controlled if it offered more of a 'just-in-time' inventory control program. I can also see the buyers' issues. I absolutely feel that I could help solve problems like this for you." Well, Steve liked that! Bridget had diagnosed a problem, and that told him that she'd really done her homework, which none of the other candidates had done.

But it was what she said at the end of the interview that impressed Steve the most. She said, "Mr. Stanasloz, I really want this job, and I want to know what I have to do to get it." She was closing the interview by asking for the job! Steve said he challenged her and asked why she wanted to work for his company. She replied, "Well, I've always given 110% at everything I do and I want to work for the best. I took the liberty of calling five of your best competitors' salespeople in the Fargo area, where the job territory is. One of your competitors' sales reps told me that the competition just follows the sales rep from your company around, in order to pick up the scraps, because that's all they can get. That's the kind of company I want to work for!"

Steve was impressed by Bridget's ability to close the sale and how she again showed him that she had really researched the industry. Steve said that none of the other candidates, good as they were, had made an impacting closing statement like Bridget's. Of course she got the job.

Note again that Bridget had stood out because she had done two things. First, she identified a problem and offered a solution. She impressed the interviewer by interviewing five buyers. Second, she made a very effective close to the interview by asking for the job and illustrated her enthusiasm by showing what she'd learned from five competitors.

How much time did it take for Bridget to get the winning edge? About two-and-a-half hours! All four candidates had invested four years and thousands of dollars in school. All four had excellent credentials. All four were "qualified." But Bridget had invested two days playing phone-tag for a total of two and a half hours of phone time to do her 10 interviews with buyers and competitors. After 12 years of school and four years of college, it was a mere two-and-a-half hours that set Bridget apart from the others.

There are lots of Bridgets out there competing for the best jobs! *You* need to be as well-prepared, better, in fact. Although her preparation was excellent, Bridget missed a golden opportunity. She should have prepared a written piece, outlining her research, to give to Steve! This would have left him with a tangible and very valuable piece of information for his company! The additional hour or two spent in writing up that sheet would have been the "nose" by which *you* could have beaten Bridget!

-Rick Nelles

Supportive Lifestyle

It's important that your career transition efforts are supported by a healthy and well-rounded lifestyle. Your career is extremely important — it's the way you earn your living, and the primary way you express yourself in the adult world. But it's not 100% of who you are. Be sure that you don't become so single-minded in your job search that you neglect other parts of your life.

❖ Pay particular attention to your **friends and family.** These are the people closest to you, and their love and support can get you through the tough times of career transition. Be sure to take time to enjoy their company.

❖ Also, make time with friends and family for **recreation and amusement.** Enjoyment of the arts, movies, books, sports, or gardening is an essential re-energizing of the soul and spirit. You'll need that in your job search campaign.

❖ One of the best things you can do for yourself is to pursue a program of **regular physical exercise.** The physical benefits are obvious, but we've found that regular exercise can increase your mental sharpness and improve your outlook.

❖ Finally, don't neglect your **spiritual needs.** During a career transition, it's important to keep your values intact and your faith strong.

Affirmation for a Supportive Lifestyle:

"As I pursue my professional goals, I never forget to pay attention to my mind, body, spirit, and my loved ones."

"It's our attitude at the beginning of a difficult undertaking which, more than anything else, will determine its outcome."
-William James, American Philosopher

Part II

Assembling Your Portfolio

- ❖ Proactive Documentation Planner
- ❖ Personal Data
- ❖ Educational Background
- ❖ Job Skills
- ❖ Recognition
- ❖ References
- ❖ Leadership
- ❖ Other Documentation

3

Proactive Documentation Planning

Now that you're all fired up, let's get at it! This section of the manual gives you step-by-step instructions on how to identify, gather and create the documentation you'll need to put together a dynamite portfolio!

Note that your **Proof of Performance Portfolio** binder contains seven dividers to help you organize your documentation. The next seven chapters each define a section of your portfolio. Each chapter will give you ideas for gathering documentation in each category. You'll discover, however, that there's a lot of potential overlap between the sections. So, you'll have the opportunity to use your judgment and creativity on where to place documentation in your portfolio.

Building your **PoP Portfolio** will consist of two primary steps:

❖ **First, you'll need to go back in your education and employment history and try to recover as many pieces of documentation as you possibly can.**

If you're a student or recent graduate, this process will be easy! You still have relationships with teachers, advisors, and coaches you worked with in school, and your employers should be readily available, so recovering or creating documentation will not be too difficult. If you've been out of school and in the workforce for several years, this process could take a while. You may be disappointed at times because you're unable to locate past documents or people who could help you. You may have misplaced your diploma, and some of your mentors may have retired or even died. Don't let this get you down! Gather what you can and focus on gathering documentation on an ongoing basis in the future.

> ❖ **Second, after you have gathered as much past documentation as possible, you will want to look forward, creating situations where you'll be able to get documentation each time you have a success. We call this process Proactive Documentation Planning.**

Proactive Planning

One of the goals of the **PoP Portfolio** is to make you a more motivated and productive employee. In your current job, you're doing more than earning a paycheck! **You're building a career,** and the quality of your results and your ability to document them can have an enormous impact on your earning potential and professional satisfaction in your next job, and the next, and the next.

> "Only those who risk going too far will ever know how far they can go."
>
> - *Good Stuff* magazine

Proactive planning means setting up specific goals for measurable or observable results with your current manager or supervisor. When you achieve a goal, ask your manager if she would be willing to provide you with a written testimonial or certificate for your portfolio commemorating that achievement.

If your manager or supervisor is curious as to why you want this documentation, explain that you're working on a **Proof of Performance Portfolio.** Let your manager know that the purpose of the portfolio is to help you document successes in your career. You might show your manager what you have assembled already. Assure your manager that you have no immediate plans to leave your job! Instead, stress how the portfolio can help both you and the manager in your current position:

> ❖ Remind your manager that he may not always be your manager, and if there is ever a change, you'll want be prepared to show a new supervisor your success rate.

> ❖ Also stress that your **PoP Portfolio** will be a very helpful tool for your yearly evaluations.

❖ Finally, you should note that in the current climate of mergers, corporate takeovers, and downsizing, you want to be prepared should things change.

Once you have set your goals, do everything you can to achieve them and **get your documentation!** You'll increase your value to your current employer, and you'll also begin to increase your value if you return to the job market. The Proactive Documentation Planner is a "win-win" proposition for you and your employer. You get proof of performance and your company gets a better, more motivated employee.

The Proactive Documentation Planner Worksheet

To help you stay organized, we've designed a form to help you plan for future documentation, but you can also use this form as you gather past documentation. By completing a worksheet for **each piece of documentation** that you want to gather, you'll be able to keep track of your progress.

The first section of the **Proactive Documentation Planner** (Form 2) is the **Accomplishment or Job Skill to Document.** If you're completing the worksheet for a past piece of documentation, simply write in the first section what you're trying to document. If this is for future documentation, write the goal or what you must accomplish to get the documentation.

You'll also see a box for the **Goal Date.** Use this box for past documentation by setting a deadline to get the documentation. For future documentation, record the date you plan to complete your goal.

Under **Forms of Documentation,** we have listed the primary types of documentation people use. You're by no means limited to these types of documentation! You should always be open to thinking of creative ways to document your successes. The list is simply to help you determine what type of documentation you're going back to get or moving forward to earn.

There is also room on the worksheet to record the **names of at least two people** who can help you get the documentation. If this is a piece of documentation that you and your manager have agreed upon, place his name as your contact.

Finally, there is a place to record when you placed the information in your **PoP Portfolio** and where you placed it.

Documentation Motivators

We suggest that, if your manager is really excited about the idea of documenting your achievement, have your manager prepare your documentation **prior to your completion of the project.** Have your manager complete all parts of the documentation except for the signature. Once you complete the project, ask your manager to sign off on the accomplishment.

Remember that not all managers are good managers and not all managers are going to see the positive benefits of the **PoP Port-folio.** All is not lost — you'll just have to work a bit harder to find other sources from whom you can gather documentation.

4

Creating Your Personal
Data PoP Documents

The Personal Data section is a very important place to begin the task of gathering documentation for your **Proof of Performance Portfolio.** Fortunately, most of the information for this section is easily accessible. It's either information that you probably already have on hand, or it is in your head, and the **PoP Portfolio** will provide a place to record that information.

Résumé

Volumes of information have been written on résumés, and there are several computer programs available to help you lay out a résumé. However, in actual practice, the only real rule for résumé-writing basically seems to be 'anything goes.' That is, whatever format you think projects you in the most positive light is the one to use. So, our focus here is not on writing résumés, but formatting a portfolio that will **back up** your résumé.

The purpose of the résumé is to set yourself apart from other candidates. We do NOT recommend using gimmicks to do this, such as cutesy graphics or wild colors. The way to set yourself apart is by providing the hiring manager with solid information that shows you're a person who not only has the basic experience, but also a **record of achievement** that will put you a cut above the other candidates.

When reading thousands of résumés, hiring managers learn to quickly review the information and identify the things they need to know. Here's a list of things most hiring managers are looking for on a résumé:

❖ **Your work history, including company name, location, dates of employment, and job title(s).**

❖ **A brief description of the company's products or services offered.** *(For salespeople, it is also important to state to whom the products or services are sold.)*

❖ **A list of things you accomplished while in that position. Accomplishments, NOT TASKS, are the most important information you can provide to a hiring manager. Your portfolio will be dedicated to supporting and documenting the claims you make in your résumé.**

❖ **Your education history, with degrees clearly identified.**

❖ Any continuing education you have completed that is appropriate for the position you're applying for.

❖ At the bottom of the résumé be sure to note: "Professional portfolio available documenting results."

Use a résumé format that uses "bullet points." Résumés written in paragraph form seldom get read. Your résumé should be in the first plastic pocket of your portfolio, and **you should carry at least five copies of your résumé with you at all times.**

Goals

Keeping a written record of your career and personal goals is a great tool for success. There's a lot of material written to help you shape your goals, but we have developed a very simple format to record these goals, called **The Proactive Career Goals Worksheet** (Form 3). Keeping this sheet in your **PoP Portfolio** and reviewing it frequently will help motivate you to achieve these goals.

Another benefit of the **Proactive Career Goals Worksheet** is that you can use it to show hiring managers your goals. You will often be asked questions in an interview that focus on your personal goals. Providing this sheet to hiring managers will assure them that you have given a lot of thought to what you're looking for in a career and that you're organized and serious.

How to complete the Proactive
Career Goals Worksheet

Dream. Dream a lot! Dream about your future life. Dream about your future jobs. Dream about your future possessions. Dream about your future family plans. Dream about your spiritual aspirations. Dream about your future finances. Dream about your future home. Dream about your retirement. A common denominator among successful people is that they dreamed big, wrote down their goals, and then went about making their dreams come true!

1. Using the left column of the worksheet, **make a list** of the things you would like in your life and career in the future. You'll find that just about every item you write under "What I Want in My Career" will have a listing opposite it under "What I Don't Want in My Career."

2. **Prioritize** the items listed in each section, using 1 for the thing you want most in a career, and in the bottom section, using 1 for the thing you want the least in a career. This will help you make career decisions.

3. In the area marked "Career Goals," **write a brief description of your dream job** and what your life will be like when you achieve your goals and begin to live your dream.

4. In the area marked "Proactive Steps to Get the Job I Want in My Career," begin writing **action steps** you need to take to achieve your dreams. This can include attitude changes as well as specific tasks.

5. In the section titled "Inactive Steps That Lead to Career Boredom," we have already compiled a list of behaviors that we have seen cripple people in the pursuit of their career goals. Add to it as you see fit.

Read your responses on a daily basis to keep yourself moving ahead!

> "When I got cut from the varsity team as a sophomore in high school, I learned something. I knew I never wanted that taste in my mouth, that hole in my stomach. So I set a goal of becoming a starter on varsity."
>
> *- Michael Jordan*

When an interviewer asks about career goals, job candidates often just make up something on the spot, trying to guess what the hiring manager would like to hear. Hiring managers can see right through this. They know you're faking it, but they can only guess what your real goals are, or whether you've ever given any real thought to your goals. The **Proactive Career Goals Worksheet** can demonstrate that you *have* given serious thought to your career and you can tell the hiring manager how this position would help you in the pursuit of your goals.

Clear Goals Are a Must

"Employers and recruiters advise job-seekers to have definite career goals that you can express clearly and enthusiastically. One recruiter refused to mince words about job-seekers who aren't sure what they want to do after graduation: 'Don't waste my time and yours.'"

- Job Outlook '99

Picture Goals

As important as it is to write your goals down, there is great power in putting your goals in pictures! By placing your picture goals on the back of your portfolio, you'll have a constant visual reminder of your goals. Some of the picture goals you may want to consider could include:

❖ **FAMILY** – Include pictures of family members or other loved ones that your success will impact.

❖ **HOUSES** – Is there a house you're dreaming to buy? Is there a second home or cabin that you want in the future? Use a picture to motivate you to work hard every day, but especially in your career transition.

❖ **THINGS** – Select pictures of material possessions that you're striving to obtain through your hard work and success. It can be a picture of a car, a set of golf clubs, clothes, jewelry, whatever motivates you to succeed.

❖ **PLACES** – Would you like to travel? Get pictures of places you would like to visit in the future.

Picture goals will become a daily reminder of your priorities and the things you are striving for in life. Visualizing your goals serves as a great way to keep your priorities before you and is one of the most effective motivators you will find!

The back of the **PoP Portfolio** has been specifically designed for you to display your picture goals. You can also include other pictures in your portfolio, but have your most important goals represented on the back cover of your portfolio.

To create a picture goals sheet, select several pictures that represent your primary goals. Crop the pictures so that they can easily fit on one sheet of paper that will fit in the back cover of the port-folio. Place the pictures on a piece of colored paper, and use a color copier to make a copy of the page for your portfolio. (*Most copy centers have affordable color copies.*) We suggest using **no more than six pictures** on the back cover.

How do you use the picture goals in the interview? First, by having your pictures on the back of the portfolio, the hiring man-ager may see the pictures and ask about them. This can be a great icebreaker for you! You can chat about some of your personal in-terests, but you can also use this as an opportunity to share briefly your ambitions for the future and how you use picture goals to motivate yourself to succeed.

Second, the hiring manager may ask you about your personal goals or priorities. The pictures are a perfect opportunity to share with the hiring manager what motivates you.

Time Management

One of the biggest errors in career transition is the poor use of time. If you're currently working full-time, efficient time manage-ment is the only way to carve out enough time for a successful job search. If you're not working, the great danger is that time is wasted by sleeping in, watching TV, and doing other meaningless activi-ties that will do little to help find your dream job.

In this book, we give you a sample of the activities that a job seeker should be doing during the job search. Most simply put,

treat the process of searching for a new job as your current job!
That means:

❖ Getting up in the morning at a regular time

❖ Showering and getting ready

❖ Getting out of the house in the morning

❖ Going to the library or copy center as if it's your
office

❖ Making phone calls in a professional manner

❖ Taking lunch breaks

❖ Wrapping up one day prepared for the next

❖ Getting plenty of rest and exercise

Your career transition should not be treated as a vacation! This
is one of the mistakes made most often in career transition.

By using a **schedule for career transition,** you will stay on task and also be able to prove to hiring managers that you have time management skills. You can use your day planner as a proof of performance. Many interviewers will be interested in your personal time management skills. If you show a hiring manager your day planner with well-written schedules and accomplishments, you'll give evidence of your ability to manage your time efficiently.

Stress Management

As we mentioned in Chapter 2, times of career transition can be some of the most stressful periods in your life. How you manage stress is a vital part of your job search, and you should document your efforts in this area. Write down your schedule for stress management activities, including exercise, recreational activities, and anything else that you're doing in this area. If a hiring manager asks you about this matter, you can show how you're coping with stress in your career transition. This information will stand you in good stead if the job you seek will involve managing your own stress or that of those working with you.

Work History

This part of the Personal Data section provides a place for you to keep track of your employment records. Every time you make a job change, be sure to update this section of your portfolio. It will save you time whenever you go through career transition, because you'll have all the information on past employers in a place that you can easily access.

The **Work History Worksheet** (Form 4) will help you keep track of important information from your past jobs. Early in your career, when you've had only a few employers, this information will be easy to remember and write down. After you've been working for 20 or 30 years you'll have to work a little harder, but the worksheet will help jog your memory. Fill in one block for each of your past jobs, making special note of your supervisor's name. Also record phone, fax and e-mail information. Having this information in one easy-to-find place will be a terrific help in your job search. It will also be helpful if you ever need to contact a past employer or manager for a reference.

Salary History

Having documentation of your salary history is an important demonstration of your value. Your salary is one indicator of your success. **By keeping your W-2s or 1099s, you can document your income from past jobs.**

Obviously, these numbers can be very important in salary negotiations! There are times when an employer may think you are overstating your past income in an attempt to get more than you are worth. By having the numbers, you can prove that you deserve the amount you're asking for.

You can use **pay stubs** to show your weekly income or to show the most you've made in a single week. Pay stubs can also give evidence of your pay period. To display these stubs, neatly mount the stubs on professional-looking paper. You can mount the W-2s and 1099s in the same way. (*1099s are especially important if you have been an independent contractor. They are the only evidence of your success!*)

Assessments

Assessments are personality tests that can be very helpful in career planning and in the interviewing process. There are many personality profiles available. We are going to recommend two that we have observed as being the most common and easily understood by hiring managers and human resources people. Before we begin discussing the profiles, we need to address one question: Why use an assessment?

❖ **Find the Right Career** – A personality assessment done early in your career search can help you identify careers that best suit your personality.

❖ **Identify Obstacles** – If you already know what career you want to pursue, the assessment can help you identify obstacles that you will need to overcome. For example, if you've decided that you want to go into sales and take a personality test, you may find out that your personality is more introverted. That doesn't mean you shouldn't seek out sales professions! You must realize, though, that your introversion may hinder your sales ability at times and that you will have to overcome that obstacle to become successful in sales.

❖ **Identify Strengths** – An assessment will do one of two things. It will confirm what you already knew about an existing strength, or it will identify a strength that you had not previously recognized in yourself. Either way, you need to find accomplishments in your life that support what the assessment identifies. **The test itself is not proof.** The results of the test **plus** past accomplishments will prove that this is a strength. If there are no results in your life to support the findings of the assessment, then you really cannot claim that trait as a strength.

❖ **Identify Weaknesses** – Many interview and résumé books try to teach you tricks to avoid exposing your weaknesses. Most successful interviewers have created ways to see through these smoke screens. It is disingenuous to believe that you do not have faults. When asked about a weakness, use the assessment to validate your weakness and then share a plan for overcoming that weakness.

❖ **Understand the Interviewer** – The profiles in most assessments will also help you identify communication styles. Understanding your profile and learning about other profiles can teach you how to better communicate with other personality types.

How to Access an Assessment

Check our website at *career-directions.com* for more information on assessments and how to purchase a personal report for you to place in your portfolio.

Recommended Assessments

DiSC®-PERSONAL PROFILE SYSTEM®

The DiSC® test is simple to take and easy to understand and will help you identify basic characteristics of your personality. The DiSC® identifies and groups human behavior in four easy-to-understand areas:

❖ Dominance

❖ Influence

❖ Steadiness

❖ Conscientiousness

Myers-Briggs Type Indicator (MBTI)

The MBTI claims to be the "most widely used personality inventory in history." It has 16 different personality profiles based on preferences on four scales:

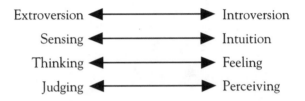

Extroversion ⬅➡ Introversion
Sensing ⬅➡ Intuition
Thinking ⬅➡ Feeling
Judging ⬅➡ Perceiving

Either of these tests can be extremely helpful. Take the information you receive from the test and display it in your portfolio with strengths and weaknesses highlighted.

Personal Mission Statement

Another helpful exercise is the creation of a Personal Mission Statement. A Personal Mission Statement can be a powerful guiding force in your life. It can give direction and focus to all of your activities and should cover both your work and personal life. You should base your Personal Mission Statement on whatever is most meaningful in your life, and you shouldn't feel limited by your present situation. Your mission statement can be, and probably will be, based on your spiritual values, although it need not be overtly religious in tone.

Your Personal Mission Statement should not be simply a description of your job or social role. "My mission is to be a great accountant" is not a good mission statement, even though the sentiment may be laudable. Your mission statement should not be a laundry list of things you want to accomplish (those are goals, not a mission statement), nor should it be full of selfish or greedy sentiments.

Your mission statement should be one sentence, easy to understand and keep in your memory. Here are some good examples of mission statements that we've come across:

❖ To recognize and utilize all the talents and grace God has given me to help others feel His love.

❖ To give my best effort in everything I set out to accomplish.

❖ To use and develop my skills to the best of my ability and to overcome my weaknesses in order to fully meet my personal potential.

Why do you need a Personal Mission Statement? A Personal Mission Statement can help you in several ways:

1. Placed in the front of your portfolio, it will serve as a daily reminder of your life mission.

2. The Personal Mission Statement serves as additional evidence of your serious forethought. Hiring managers love to work with people who know where they want to go in life.

3. The Personal Mission Statement can help keep you on track when confronted with career decisions. When looking at opportunities, you should look at your Personal Mission Statement to be sure the opportunity is consistent with who you want to become.

Additional Help

For more on creating mission statements, look at one or both of the following books. Stephen R. Covey's *Seven Habits of Highly Effective People* can help you create a very detailed mission statement. Laurie Beth Jones's *The Path: Creating Your Mission Statement for Work and Life* is a fairly brief book that can help you put together a simple but powerful mission statement.

5

Documenting Your Educational Background

Where is your college diploma? Is it on your wall, stuffed away in a drawer, tucked in the pages of a book? *Have you lost it?* Where are the transcripts that show your course grades and your G.P.A.? Do you have an advanced degree, or have you completed some other educational program? Keep copies of all your educational documents in your **Proof of Performance Portfolio**! You'll always be able to produce them in your portfolio when you are asked about your education.

The Education section of your **PoP Portfolio** should be one of the easiest sections to build. Simply dig around in your stuff and pull out your diplomas, transcripts, award certificates, yearbooks, and other documents from school. If you have misplaced some of these documents, you should contact the schools or organizations and have duplicates made. This may cost you a little money, but it's a small investment to make your **Proof of Performance Portfolio** more effective and complete!

Diplomas

At the end of most educational programs, you are given a diploma, certificate, or some other kind of documentation to prove your successful completion. You've probably stuck those sheets in a drawer somewhere, or you may have framed them for display in your home or office. Don't put the original documents in your **PoP Portfolio,** as they're too fragile and too valuable. Instead, **make color copies of your diplomas.** If your diploma is smaller than 8½" x 11", mount the copy on a piece of paper, preferably one that complements the colors in your diploma. If it's larger, have it reduced to fit the 8½" x 11" format. *(If you've completed a level of education beyond high school, you may not need to include your high school diploma. Still, your **PoP Portfolio** is a good place to keep your high school diploma so that it is never lost.)* You should also include diplomas for the completion of vocational education, if such education is important to the career you're pursuing.

You may not need to show your diplomas in every interview, but they're important to have. As you share your educational experiences, show the appropriate diploma as proof of your educational accomplishment. It leaves no doubt in a hiring manager's mind that you have the education they need!

Grades

You should **get a transcript of your grades** and include a copy in your **Proof of Performance Portfolio.** If you were on the Dean's List, give your transcript a prominent place in your portfolio! But even if grades weren't your strong point, you should put a transcript somewhere in your portfolio. They are the grades you earned, and you should have access to that information.

It's Not All Academic

Good grades are important, but potential employers also value work experience and extracurricular activities. "Employers look at candidates who have some experience in the work world as better able to make that move [from campus to career] and better prepared to accept the responsibilities of the job....Recruiters also cited involvement in campus activities, especially those that provide the student with a chance to play a leadership role, as a way candidates can demonstrate their ability to handle responsibility."

- Job Outlook '99

You can mount your grade reports neatly on colored paper. Highlight grades that are particularly relevant to the position you are applying for. Again, if you have completed any post-secondary education, you may not need to display your high school grades.

If your grades aren't impressive, you may not want to volunteer the information in an interview, but as a recent graduate and early in your career, grades will be one of the proofs of performance that you will be asked for most often. You will not be able to dodge this question! You can use the information to show the interviewer that you are an honest person who takes responsibility for your past performance.

One thing that can help offset less-than-spectacular grades is showing that you were employed full-time during college. It's even more impressive if you're able to show you earned 100 percent of your college expenses!

Informational interviewing can also help a great deal if your grades aren't great. If you've conducted informational interviews with people who know that particular hiring manager, then you may be able to find out how important grades are to the hiring manager.

Extracurricular Activities

Especially if you don't have strong grades, be sure to **document your college activities!** Include programs from music, theater, or dance performances, sports events, debate competitions, and anything that lists you as the recipient of an award. If you have pictures, include them! You can also photocopy pages from your yearbook that substantiate your participation. Many hiring managers will rate extracurricular programs, which demand a great deal of time and dedication, more important than grades! Another reason to document your activities is that a lot of people lie about their involvement in extracurriculars, and hiring managers know it. Your ability to document your involvement gives you a distinct advantage.

Honors

Graduating from high school as a member of the National Honor Society or graduating from college *summa cum laude, magna cum laude,* or as a Phi

Beta Kappa member is unquestionable recognition of your educational success. It sets you apart from other job candidates. **Include copies of these honors** in your portfolio, as well as any other academic citations, such as departmental commendations. If you can find one, a picture of you receiving the award can make a great impact on a hiring manager.

Certificates

During school, and especially during your career, you often have the opportunity to get additional education and training. Examples might include courses in computer software, tax preparation, or business writing. When you complete such a training program, you'll usually get a certificate from the trainer, recognizing that you completed the training and are certified in some area of skill. Include copies of all such certificates in your **PoP Portfolio**. If they didn't give you a certificate, you might include some illustrative piece of work from the course to document your participation.

Continuing and Professional Education, Seminars, Etc.

In many professions, continuing education is a necessary part of keeping your professional license. In many states, real estate salespeople, insurance agents, educators, and accountants, to name just a few, must continually take classes to stay current in their profession. Include documentation of any relevant classes and seminars you have completed and place them in your **Proof of Performance Portfolio**!

6

Identifying and Documenting Your Job Skills

In this chapter, you'll learn how to document your job skills, especially those that hiring managers are most interested in. This may be the most important section in the portfolio, as it will be used to answer many questions in the interview.

Communication Skills

If you peruse the want ads, you'll notice that many positions—even those that aren't in the communications industry—are advertised as requiring "excellent oral and written communication skills." So it's probably accurate to say that **whatever your career goal, you're going to have to demonstrate your ability to communicate** effectively to the hiring manager! Your **spoken communication skills** will be judged primarily by your interactions with the hiring manager and his staff: that is, telephone conversations and especially in the formal job interview. If you have a particular skill or training in spoken communication, you should document that fact, either in this section, or the education section, or both.

In Chapter 14, "Preparing for the Formal Interview," you'll find some exercises that you can do to improve your telephone and interview skills. These will help you stay in top form. Your past skills and training are fine, and documentation is important, but they are all worthless unless you **continually exercise your spoken communication skills throughout the entire hiring process!**

Wanted: Good Communicators!

"Year after year, recruiters have said they want to hire good communicators. Communication skills top their list of what characteristics they value in job candidates."

The top seven communication skills employers sought were:

1. Interpersonal
2. Teamwork
3. Verbal communication
4. Analytical
5. Computer
6. Written communication
7. Leadership

- Job Outlook '99

Written Communication

There are many ways to document your writing skills. By far **the most impressive documentation is material that has been published:** books, magazine and journal articles, newsletter stories, and the like.

These are effective because they represent a third party's validation of your writing skill. If you haven't had anything published — and even if you have — you may want to include writing samples from other sources. Here's a list of ideas:

❖ Excerpts from college term papers

❖ Articles submitted for publication (but not accepted)

❖ Instruction or training manuals you've contributed to

❖ Brochures you have developed

❖ Advertising copy

❖ Marketing pieces and letters

❖ Business letters

❖ Research reports

❖ Summaries from informational interviewing and other narratives written in the **PoP Portfolio**

Be sure that all samples of your writing are the highest quality! Don't include something that's been published if you don't think it's your best work. If you're uneasy about your writing, have someone who can recognize good writing skills examine any pieces you decide to include in the portfolio.

Demonstrating Organizational Skills

Proof of organizational skills made all the difference for Gary Sabourin! Gary was interviewing for a sales position with a top-billing FM radio station located in Minneapolis. Competition was fierce, and Gary didn't have as much experience as many of the over 100 other candidates seeking the position. It was obvious that it would take something significant to beat out the competition.

Gary had been a trainer for a world-class shot-putter, and had designed a program that led the athlete to become one of the top ten in the world. Gary wrote the program down in a black book planner. "Activities" and "Results" were written down daily, in meticulous detail. Gary shared the training book with the hiring manager.

In the final interview, the interviewer spent nearly ten minutes reviewing the plan and Gary's detailed records! He loved the demonstration of Gary's organizational skills and his commitment to work a plan. The interviewer handed the book back and congratulated him on getting the job!

Thank You Notes and Cover Letters

Although they aren't actually a part of your **Proof of Performance Portfolio,** your cover letter and the thank-you note you write as a follow-up to your interview are two very important places where you can show off your writing skills. Remember that your cover letter may well get you the interview and, eventually, the job. You want it to be as perfect as you can make it, because it will probably form the first impression the hiring manager has of you. Conversely, the thank-you note you send after the interview will form a lasting impression, so you'll want to carefully craft your thank-you note to reflect the tone of your interview and the personality of the interviewer. We have a special section in Chapter 14, "Preparing for the Formal Interview," about these two important pieces of written communication.

Organizational Skills

Your ability to organize yourself, a project, your co-workers, or any other activity is one of the most important skills that an employer will be looking for. The fact that you come into the interview with your **Proof of Performance Portfolio** will in itself be good evidence to the hiring manager that you're a well-organized person! Of course, every profession requires unique organizational expertise, and you will be using the information you gather from informational interviews to identify those skills specific to your chosen career. Nevertheless, **here are several generic ar-**

eas, common to almost every industry, that you can document to prove your organizational skills:

1. **Project Management** – Bring in documentation of the initial plan of a project you were in charge of, and show what you accomplished. Include letters from members of the project team and your supervisor, giving testimony that your management of the project was one of the important factors contributing to its successful completion.

2. **Self Management** – Many times, your own personal management can be documented by your own day organizer. If you keep good records in your day organizer, show that as documentation of your organizational skills. A well-organized briefcase or attaché case with extra résumés, your portfolio, a notepad, extra pens, and thank-you cards will also be an impressive display of your own personal organization.

3. **Personal Job Evaluations** – Past job evaluations will probably address all aspects of your work, but if they stress your organizational skills, be sure to highlight those comments. If you have mislaid a past evaluation and you're still on good terms with your former supervisor, by all means contact him to see if he would

be willing to pull out a copy of the evaluation from his files and send you a copy.

Platform Skills

Platform skills include **public speaking, presentation, and the ability to lead meetings.** This isn't essential for every position, but in some jobs it's an absolute necessity, and it can be a difficult skill to document. If you need documentation on your platform skills, you'll need to get creative! Here are some suggestions of pieces that capture this documentation:

❖ Program from the event listing you as presenter

❖ Videotape of the presentation

❖ Pictures of the presentation

❖ Evaluations from people who were at your presentation

❖ Evaluations completed by your supervisor

❖ Results of the presentation

Training Skills

Training can range from working with a single person to presenting to a large group and can be for fellow employees or for clients. Documentation of your training skills will be needed in two primary areas:

Program Development - The development of curriculum and all other aspects of a training program. Documentation might consist of:

❖ A copy of the course syllabus or outline, showing how the course was scheduled, and the material that was covered in each session

❖ A statement of the goals of the course, and how students would demonstrate that they had successfully completed the training

❖ Samples of materials used in the class, whether you used an existing program, or, especially, if you developed the materials yourself

❖ Facilities or location where the class was held, on site or in a remote location, and the role the facility played in the training

❖ The methodology or philosophy on which you built the training program

Program Results ‑ Focusing on the outcome of the training. Many people can develop a training program, but this documents your success. Areas of results could include:

❖ A definition of the course objectives and the percentage of students who successfully completed the course

❖ Turnover rates of people who completed the courses

❖ An increase in production by people trained with your program

❖ Positive changes in the corporate culture that are a direct result of the training

❖ Student evaluations

❖ Evaluations by superiors

Conflict Resolution

Conflict is a regular occurrence at many places of employment. How you've been able to handle that conflict is one of the most important skills you can document for future employers. Your ability to cooperate with others and get results can be a significant contributor to your winning the job! **This is an area where a story would be a great piece of documentation.** Identify a specific time when you were able to bring resolution to a conflict. Write the story, including these details:

❖ Positions of the people involved, and how their position interacted with your position

❖ The source of the conflict

❖ What problems the conflict was causing

❖ Your role in the situation

❖ How you resolved the conflict

❖ The positive results of your efforts

By writing the story, you'll be able to capture the details that make the story more credible, and you can also practice telling the story in an interview.

Budget Planning

The ability to develop and manage a budget is important in many jobs and in every position of leadership. Budgeting ability can be easily demonstrated if you've taken care to keep excellent records — and as a good budget manager, you'll have done so! **Document your ability to manage a budget by showing your initial budget and then a year-end accounting of the results.** *(Be sure, however, that you don't use any proprietary information from your former employer when you do this.)*

If you've never been responsible for a budget in a work situation, then document the financial responsibility you have had in an organization or club! Even if you haven't had work experience in this area, do your best to document how you've used this skill in other positions of responsibility. As with all other job skill areas, a testimonial from a former supervisor about your budgetary expertise is always a good document to include in your portfolio.

Sales

One of the most important professions in which to document your success is in sales. Much of the need for this book resulted from our work in recruiting sales professionals. We discovered that it was difficult to identify whether a salesperson was productive, just from an interview. We began to notice that top sales producers were coming in with good documentation that left little doubt about their past performance!

Nearly every hiring manager we've worked with in the sales profession has told us that **past performance is the number one concern when evaluating a potential candidate in sales.** We encourage candidates to gather documentation to support their claims, because candidates who do the work of documenting are amazed at how much better their results are in getting good job offers! Here are some items you can use to document your past sales success:

❖ Awards and recognition for being Salesperson of the Month, Quarter, or Year

❖ Published rankings that show you in the top 20 percent of all performers

❖ Records documenting your ability to cold call

❖ Testimonials from customers revealing how your sales ability has benefited their company

❖ Documentation that shows your record against assigned quotas and/or goals

❖ Documentation that shows the growth of sales in your territory

❖ Daily records or reports of activity

❖ Copies of large invoices or contracts for major accounts

❖ Closing ratios

❖ Customer lists

❖ Stories about how you won your biggest account

❖ Stories about an account you had to work extra hard to get

❖ Stories about how you saved an account that was dissatisfied

Marketing

There are many different aspects to marketing. You will need to customize your **Proof of Performance Portfolio** to suit the specialization you're pursuing. For example, if the area of marketing you are interested in is advertising, then the portfolio will be a creative place for you to advertise yourself! Your entire portfolio should demonstrate the creative flair that you would use in promoting a product or service, as well as the ads, commercials, or ad campaigns you have created.

Management

Management provides many opportunities to demonstrate your ability to perform. In assembling your documentation, your goal will be to **identify the accomplishments that are most important to your ongoing career.** Here's a list of potential factors to document. *(Note that many of the skills we've already identified will overlap this section.)*

❖ Project management

❖ Training and developing employees

❖ Interviewing, hiring, and dismissing employees

❖ Confronting and correcting subordinates constructively

❖ Turnover rates

❖ Problem solving

❖ Work reviews

❖ Thank-you letters from superiors or clients

❖ Customer references or testimonials

❖ Implementing policy and procedures

❖ Inventory control

Team Participation

Being a part of a team is becoming a more common workplace circumstance than ever before. Many projects are far too big for an individual person, and demand a staff of people who each have specialization in a specific area. This is increasingly true for those who are going into information systems careers. There are many ways to document your positive participation. Following are some creative ideas for showing your involvement:

❖ Get testimonials from the team leader or from fellow team members about your participation.

❖ Include a clipping from a company newsletter about your team and its project.

❖ Take a picture of the team and place it alongside the story of the project.

❖ Show how the project produced results for the company.

Punctuality

It doesn't matter how good you are at your job, if you're not there, nothing gets done. Attendance and punctuality are important ingredients in any employee, but are even more important for the recent graduate: college classes don't always foster healthy attendance habits! Students are often allowed to pick and choose when to attend classes, and many summer and part-time jobs tolerate poor attendance and tardiness because of the lack of people available for the job.

When seeking the best jobs, there is no allowance for poor attendance or lack of punctuality. Be sure that you have an excellent track record in your summer and part-time jobs. Document these traits in your **PoP Portfolio** through a recommendation letter or testimonial.

Counseling

We're not talking here about professional counseling. Nobody expects you to be a therapist or a social worker — unless, of course, that's your chosen career! Instead, we're talking about the many job situations where there's a need for helping fellow employees. This can involve mentoring a new worker, helping someone successfully navigate a difficult situation, or assisting someone with a serious personal problem that is affecting his job performance. Obviously, this area may have overlap with training, conflict resolution, and several areas of management. Nevertheless, if you feel that this is a particular strength for you, you should stress it in your **PoP Portfolio.**

The subjective and sometimes confidential nature of counseling makes it one of the most difficult but important areas of documentation. Many people claim to be counselors, but not everyone is able to get the positive results that demonstrate their ability to counsel. The best documentation will come from people whom you have helped and from supervisors who can attest to your positive contribution in this area.

Re-Engineering

You don't have to be an actual engineer to have skill in this area. "Re-Engineering" is just a fancy newfangled term for reorganizing something in a comprehensive way. As a separate skill, it would apply to any experience you've had in totally reorganizing a department, division, or even an entire company.

Documentation for this skill could include company charts or lists showing the organizational structure of the unit before and after your re-engineering project. Testimonials from your supervisors would also be effective proof of your achievement in this important and difficult area of skill.

7

Maximizing Your Recognition Documents

This chapter is short and sweet, because the documentation we cover here will be pretty easy to gather! Many organizations are very good at recognizing accomplishments by employees. This recognition can come in a variety of ways. If you've received some of the types of recognition discussed below, you probably still have them around.

Awards

Awards are one of the most popular types of recognition. Many organizations present awards to employees for outstanding accomplishments. Types of awards might include:

❖ Trophies

❖ Plaques

❖ Pins

❖ Rings

❖ Medals

❖ Certificates

The problem with most of these awards is that they're meant to be hung on the wall or displayed on a shelf. This makes it pretty hard to take them with you on an interview—although we have heard stories of candidates lugging a box full of awards into the interview with them! We have a better idea for displaying your awards: **simply have pictures taken of them and display these pictures in your Proof of Performance Portfolio** in the Recognition section.

Tips for Pictures and Awards

The best picture you can get is one of **you accepting the award.** It will be impossible to go back and capture past moments, but for the future, we suggest that you always have a camera at any awards ceremony. It is important to capture the excitement of the moment. The next best picture is simply of **the award itself.** We'd suggest taking your awards to a professional photographer and have them take the pictures. This will cost a little, but it's essential that you be able to read any inscriptions on the award, and a pro knows how to light inanimate objects. The quality will be worth it. (*If you shoot the picture yourself, be sure to fill the frame up with the award. Get as close as you can to the award when shooting the picture and be sure the lighting is right.*) A simple picture of **you with the award** is nice but probably not as effective as the previous two ideas.

Have the picture blown up to at least 5"x7", but preferably 8"x10". It also may be a nice touch to have the picture matted with a lightweight mat that fits in the plastic sleeve. It's also beneficial to have a story (see Chapter 8) to go with the picture of the award. Over the course of time, it's possible to forget some of the details of how and why you won the award.

If you have a pin or other award jewelry, you may decide to wear it to the interview, as long as it's tasteful. Otherwise, shoot a super close-up photograph. Certificates, of course, are easy: remove them from their frames and make color copies of them, matte them if you wish, and place them in a protective plastic sleeve in your portfolio.

Avocational Recognition vs. Career Recognition

As you develop documentation for the **PoP Portfolio**, you'll find two main sources for documentation. The first source is your past employment history, and the second source is non-work activities that you have been involved with. These include sports, clubs, volunteer organizations, charitable events—any activity outside of your job.

It's fine to use documentation from these activities in your portfolio. But remember that documentation from these activities is not as powerful as documentation from a former job. Use documentation from avocational activities as secondary support, or when you don't have employment-related documentation for a certain job skill or accomplishment.

Right after graduation and early in your career, you'll have trouble creating documentation from the workplace, simply because of your lack of experience. The same goes if you are shifting into a brand-new career and you're trying to show that you have skills that will transfer to your new profession. In those cases, it's just fine to use your extracurricular and avocational activities to provide documentation.

Prizes

Prizes are often given for recognition. The difference between prizes and awards is simple: an award is a tangible commemorative object that you can keep forever. A prize is consumable; that is, it's something of value that you use up. Examples of prizes are trips, gift certificates, special privileges, tickets, and cash bonuses. How do you document these prizes? Once again, the camera is your best friend.

Tips for Documenting Prizes

❖ As with awards, it's great to have a picture of you actually receiving the prize.

❖ If you win a trip, be sure to take pictures on the trip, and if it's a company trip with other achievers, get a group shot.

❖ Gift certificates are sometimes difficult to document. We suggest that you take pictures at the restaurant or store that the gift certificates are for. A picture of you in front of the establishment holding the certificates may also be effective.

❖ For special privileges, you need to be creative. One example of a special privilege is a real estate sales company that allowed the monthly sales leader to drive a company-rented Saab convertible. A great picture of this privilege would be one of you behind the wheel with your best smile.

❖ Be sure to take good pictures and mount them attractively in your portfolio.

❖ Write a story to go along with each picture or have a testimonial letter from a supervisor.

Published Articles and Memos

Many accomplishments are recorded in company newsletters or magazines. Any time your name is mentioned in an article, be sure to get a copy of that publication! Display the article and its source in your **PoP Portfolio.**

At times, a memo is the only written mention of your accomplishments. Be sure to save any memo that recognizes you for an accomplishment, and mount it in your portfolio!

8

Gathering References
That Make an Impact

Most candidates come to an interview armed only with a résumé. On the bottom of the résumé they will note that references are "available upon request." That is standard procedure, and there is nothing wrong with it. However, if you use that standard line you lose an incredible opportunity to impress the interviewer with your job skills and talents. **We recommend that you have no fewer than three reference letters when you enter the formal interview.** The reference letters are then able to enhance the presentation of your qualifications. Have you ever heard of a salesperson making a sales call without some form of documentation that validates the quality of the product or service? A résumé alone can never have this kind of impact.

How to Develop and Gather
Reference Letters that Sizzle

Many reference letters that we see are flat and say little to excite a hiring manager. The majority of reference letters speak only of general personality traits: "John is a reliable worker," "Mary gets along well with her peers," and so forth. This tells the hiring manager very little, and it's usually just dumb luck if something in this kind of letter has any impact. When requesting a reference letter, **you should ask the letter writer to refer to specific accomplishments and tasks that you have completed. What you're seeking is a performance reference, rather than a simple character reference.** Most people have trouble formulating a reference letter, and they will appreciate your help in reminding them of the things you have accomplished, especially if they haven't worked with you for a while.

Here's how you go about getting a really good letter of reference: let the person know that you will be using his letter in your **Proof of Performance Portfolio** and that it should be addressed "To Whom It May Concern." Explain what the portfolio is all about. You may want to show them what you've compiled already. Make it clear that the letter you're requesting will be seen by many different interviewers and, of course, you'll see the letter yourself. (*This differs from a letter written in support of an application for a specific position. In that case, you would provide the writer with a stamped envelope to send the letter directly to the hiring manager at the company where you're applying, and you would never see the letter unless the writer provided you with a copy.*)

After someone has agreed to write a reference letter for you, tell him that you'll **send him an example reference letter,** and if he would prefer, he could use your example and copy it on his letterhead. In your example, mention specific things you accomplished while you worked or studied with them. Make it clear, of course, that they should feel free to alter your example letter as they see fit.

It's remarkable how many people really do appreciate having an example to work from, and there's nothing "pushy" or pretentious about making suggestions about the content of the letter. Finally, you should always send a special thank-you note along with your reference examples.

Go out of your way to make things convenient for them. Print your example reference letter with at least a two-inch margin at the top, to allow space for their letterhead. We suggest that you send the letter in a #10 envelope and include a self-addressed stamped #9 envelope for them to use to return the reference letter to you. People are very busy, and this will help them return the letter to you more conveniently. (*#9 envelopes are less common than #10, but office supply stores have them. They will fit nicely inside a #10 and will still hold a business-size letter. This arrangement looks much more professional than folding up a return envelope.*)

Once you receive the reference letter back, **make at least two color copies of the reference letter.** Always make color copies! Black and white copies look cheap and do not have the impact of color. Take one copy of the reference letter and highlight specific items that you believe point out your skills and talents quickly. You will be leaving this copy behind with your résumé in the interview. Now you'll be able to use the reference letters effectively in the interviewing process. Take time to study each letter, to make sure you know its contents and in what situations you will want to use it.

Saved by a Jerk

Samantha L. related this experience to us—

"As a new college graduate, I found myself on the 41st floor of a big office building, talking to a recruiter who was asking me some really tough questions. I wondered why this guy was so intense! He demanded to know my three strongest skills, and where my proof of performance was. He asked me what things I should bring to an interview. He wanted me to provide detailed stories to show that I was assertive and that I had overcome obstacles. He said, 'Tell me about a time when you went above and beyond the call of duty.' It was question after question, and at the end, he gave me a bunch of assignments: assembling references, practicing a two-minute 'commercial' about myself, and so forth.

"On my way home, I thought, 'What a jerk! I'm not going back and I'm not going to do all those assignments.' Two days later, the 'jerk' called me! He told me that he had set up an interview for me. He told me a lot of good things about the company and the job was right up my alley—a lot of things in my background and experience really applied. Then he asked how I was coming on the assignments. I said I hadn't done much. He was patient with me, but pretty much demanded that if I was going to interview with one of his clients, I'd better be prepared! So I went to my summer employers and got letters of reference. I did exactly what I was told to do, including practicing my 'two-minute commercial' and my closing statement. I really worked hard at it.

Well, I went into that interview and blew them away! I ended up securing a great job as a result of my extra efforts, and I never would have gotten that job if I hadn't run into that 'jerk' who gave me a slap in the face about what the business world is really like.

You can't just go in and wing it! You've got to know who you are, what your strengths and weaknesses are, and how to you present yourself. Don't go in unprepared!

Testimonials

Testimonials vary slightly from reference letters. **A testimonial letter focuses on a specific accomplishment,** while a reference letter may cover several accomplishments in more general terms. Testimonials can be gathered immediately after accomplishments occur.

People other than your immediate supervisor can write testimonial letters. Customers, co-workers, clients, or any other person who directly observed or benefited from your efforts can write testimonial letters. These letters can make just as big an impact as a letter from your supervisor! Many times, your supervisor does not see your day-to-day activities. For a testimonial letter to be effective, it should do the following:

❖ Explain your relationship to the person writing the testimonial

❖ Identify when this accomplishment took place

❖ Tell what was accomplished

❖ Describe your role in the process

❖ Show how you made a difference in the situation

❖ Be signed and dated and contain an address and a phone number

Testimonials become more impressive the higher the title of the person who signs the testimonial. Also, the size of the company or account influences the impact of the testimonial.

Work Reviews

Most employees have either annual, semiannual, or quarterly reviews. Whenever possible, **get a copy of your work review!** Then make at least one copy of your review and place it in your **Proof of Performance Portfolio**. Highlight the most impressive areas of your review.

Once you've left your current company, it will be difficult to go back and get this information. Furthermore, you may be unable to get a reference letter from that company, so your performance reviews may be your only documentation that can prove your performance.

Stories

Another unique way to document your past performance, which will also prepare you for an interview, is to write stories about your past performance. In the current interviewing environment, many companies are using "behavioral" interviewing methods. Behavioral interviews use questions that ask you to recall your past actions in specific situations. For example, an interviewer might ask, "Tell me about a time when you were able to take a dissatisfied customer and make them a satisfied customer." A statement like this is asking for a specific response. You must go back into your past and give an example. The interviewer does not want to know what you *would* do or *should* do, but what you **have done** in the past.

> Success is to be measured not so much by the position that one has reached in life as by the obstacles that one has overcome while trying to succeed.
>
> *- Booker T. Washington*

Behavioral interviewing is designed to help the interviewer discover proof of your past performance. The interviewer knows that **your past performance is the best indicator of your future performance.** By preparing stories before you enter the interview, you will be better able to relate those stories in response to the appropriate question. Stories do not necessarily need to have someone sign off on them. It is helpful, though, to include names of people and companies involved in the story. The more details you include, the more powerful the story will be. In writing a story, you have the further advantage of using your own words, rather than relying on the words of someone writing a testimonial for you.

And you should **write the stories down**! Don't just go over them in your mind. When you write the stories down, you'll have better command of the details. Many times candidates who have not written out their stories and practiced telling them will "freeze up" in the interview process. There's nothing that will kill the momentum of a good interview quicker than being asked a question and giving the hiring manager the "deer in the headlights" look! The whole purpose of the **PoP Portfolio** is to prepare you in every way for the interview.

How to Prepare a Story for Your Portfolio

First of all, you should be constantly looking for opportunities to do a story! It can come from either your work or volunteer activities, just as long as it's a powerful proof of your skill in some job-related area. Once you've settled on an idea, you should organize your story:

❖ Identify what the project was, and your role in it.

❖ Write the story in a business-like but engaging first-person style. Include as much quantification as you can.

❖ Include a picture if possible, showing you and the members of the group of people involved.

❖ Get someone to validate the story with a brief letter, targeted to the specific skill you wish to illustrate. Make this as convenient as possible for the person. You will probably write the testimonial yourself and ask the person to simply sign off on it.

❖ Put the story together so it will fit on a single page. Use graphics and color tastefully and for maximum impact. Most computer programs can do an acceptably professional-looking job with these stories — you needn't go crazy hiring a graphic designer or anything like that!

❖ See the sample story we've prepared on the Elk River High School Band fund-raising project (page 188).

Remember that résumés do not impact people the way this type of information will. Some interviewers will even want a copy of the story to show other people involved in the interviewing process. Never forget that hiring managers interview many candidates. It's hard for them to remember each candidate, especially after a couple of days have passed. A copy of your story will help them better recall your specific talents and skills. Having this information will help immensely when the hiring manager wants to tell someone else about your qualifications.

9

Wanted: Leaders To Lead

All employers are looking for leaders. Employers want people who are able to inspire others and show them direction, people who can challenge others to go beyond the status quo and exceed their own expectations, people who can make a difference! **If you can document your successes in leadership, you'll gain a substantial competitive advantage in the job market,** because even though most entry-level positions are not leadership positions, companies are looking for people with leadership potential for the future.

This section of your **Proof of Performance Portfolio** is designed specifically for you to document your accomplishments in positions of leadership. Most people fail to take advantage of their leadership experience. They simply make reference to leadership positions on their résumé. They seldom list their accomplishments in those positions. Here's how to get maximum impact out of your past leadership positions. There are many environments in which you can document your leadership skills:

❖ Work

❖ School

❖ Athletics

❖ Clubs

❖ Community organizations

❖ Professional organizations

❖ Charitable events

This list is not comprehensive. There are many other areas in which you can document your leadership skills. Be sure to write down any other areas you can think of!

What Should I Document?

Many people think it's impressive that they simply achieved and held a leadership position, but this actually proves very little. What is impressive is what you accomplish while in that leadership role. Leadership positions vary from organization to organization, so **look back at every leadership position you've held, and determine what the organization accomplished under your leadership.** Here's a list of potential accomplishments:

❖ Fund-raising efforts that surpassed previous years

❖ New successful fund-raisers that were developed

❖ Successful membership drives

❖ Community outreach projects

❖ Successful public relations campaigns

❖ Accomplishment of specific organizational goals

❖ Improved public awareness of your group or organization

❖ Ongoing success of the organization after you left

You can document your successful leadership skills in many ways:

❖ Letters and testimonials from board members, other officers, or faculty advisers

❖ Articles from organizational newsletters

❖ Newspaper stories

❖ Certificates of accomplishment

❖ Pictures with a story

❖ Testimonials from other members of the group

The ideas listed above are fairly obvious, so look for other creative ways to document your success! Always remember that **the most important thing to do in documenting your leadership experience is to show that your leadership produced results.** Leadership without results is not leadership!

10

Other Documentation

There's no way that we could ever cover every form of documentation possible. Every job has its own particular profile. Every person has his own individual set of experiences, skills, and personality characteristics. The possibilities for the **Proof of Performance Portfolio** are infinite! Just as no two people are the same, no two portfolios will ever be the same.

Use this section of the **PoP Portfolio** to display pieces of documentation that do not fit anywhere else in the portfolio—things that pertain specifically to your chosen career, and things that highlight your unique background and capabilities.

Part III

Your Job-Seeking Campaign

❖ Researching

❖ Networking

❖ Informational Interviewing

❖ Preparing for the Formal Interview

❖ Using Your Portfolio in the Interview

11

Researching the Job Market

Now that you're well on your way to assembling a powerful portfolio to document your accomplishments, it's time to think about your job-seeking campaign. In this section, we'll cover researching, networking, and informational interviewing Finally, we'll talk about preparing for the formal job interview where you land your dream job!

In reality, of course, you'll probably be doing a lot of these things concurrently. As you build your portfolio, you'll be doing some research, and as you ask for reference letters and testimonials, you'll be creating a network of folks who can help you in your career transition. Whether you realize it or not, when you make these contacts, you're conducting "informational interviews." And although we tend to think of the formal interview as the very last part of the process, you never know when one of your contacts might invite you to interview for a position that has just opened up! For clarity's sake, however, we'll be going topic-by-topic, starting with some very important homework: research.

Research can help you in your choice of career, your choice of industry, and, ultimately, your choice of which company you'd like to work for. Strange as it may seem, few people take the trouble to learn any details about the career they are pursuing! They simply guess what the job and the company will be like, and then they're often disappointed when faced with the day-to-day routines of the job or an unpleasant company culture.

(We'll be discussing industry and company research here. We're assuming that your college major, your internships, and your part-time work have steered you in a career direction, or, for career-changers, that you've given considerable thought to your new career. If you're completely in the dark about what you'd like to do, we suggest that you look over one or more of the excellent books available on choosing a career.)

As you'll learn in Chapter 13, the most valuable source of information about industries and companies comes from informational interviewing. Doing some basic preliminary research can help you to narrow your focus, so that you can target the industries, the companies, and, eventually, the individual people you'd like to contact. Background research can help you take fullest advantage of your informational interviews.

Your Research Will Show

"More than half of the respondents [in a recent survey of employers] said they were impressed by candidates who do their research prior to a job interview and know about the company and the position. Others...said that candidates who can ask pertinent, intelligent questions in the interview leave their mark.

"Employers recommend that students research potential companies by attending information sessions and career fairs, surfing web sites, reading company brochures, and talking to current employees. 'Research the company so you can ask questions. Know as much as possible about the position for which you are interviewing and relate your own skills and experience directly to the position'"

- Job Outlook '99

Researching Companies

Every career book you read and every career counselor you talk to will tell you to research the companies you are interested in. What they don't always tell you is how to research and what you are looking for. Here's some of the information you'll want to find, and how you can use it as you prepare for an interview. (*If you're a recent graduate, research techniques will be familiar to you. If you've been away from academia for some time, you might need to brush up on your fact-finding skills, and maybe even learn some new ones, such as "surfing the Net.")*

Company Profiles

You should probably start by looking for basic information on a company in general-interest newspapers and magazines, as well as in industry journals. News reports on a company can tell you something about its corporate culture, its record as a corporate citizen, its employee relations, its future prospects, and possible areas of concern. From these basic profiles, you'll be able to decide, based on your own ambitions and values, whether you want to learn more about the company.

Research Can Take Your Résumé to the Top of the Pile

While I was the Corporate Recruiting Manager for C.H. Robinson Company I represented our company at a job fair, and out of 120 resumes submitted, there was only one person there who really stood out. Like most of the other candidates, he was courteous and professional, and he thanked me for the opportunity to interview. But what made him unique was that he was the only person who had done any solid research on our company.

He had gone to the library and photocopied an article about our company, and he highlighted some pertinent facts about our company. He said, "Your company has risen to the top because you know how to handle freight with a sense of urgency." He felt that this gave our company a competitive edge, and said that we were the kind of company he wanted to work for.

When I returned to my office a week later, faced with reviewing 120 résumés, this man's résumé stood out from the rest, because I had attached the article he brought with him. I immediately remembered his face and our conversation. He was the only candidate invited back for a second and third interview and was hired. His research was what made him stand out from the crowd.

-Rick Nelles

Products and Services

Find out as much as possible about the products and services that the company offers. Which ones are the most important to the company's growth? Which ones are most important to the company's customers? Which are new, and which are in development?

Financial Background

You'll want to look into the company's finances. Growth in sales is the first thing to look for, as this is always a good indicator of the company's strength. If there is no growth, you'll want to ask about that in an interview. For example, you may ask, "Why have sales been stagnant for the past five years?" The answer to this question will provide you with better understanding of the company's stablility and future potential. This is a question you could not have asked without doing research!

Competitor Information

Gathering information on a company's competitors will help you to see where the company is positioned in its industry. You'll be able to identify whether the company you're interviewing with has a lot of tough competition, whether it's an industry leader, or whether it's a new and growing force in the industry.

Personnel

Check thoroughly to see if there has been any press coverage on anyone working at the company. Has the person you are interviewing with, or the person you will be working for, been written up in a magazine, journal, or newspaper? Get a copy of that article! There can be a time to use it in the formal interview. It compliments the interviewer and proves you did your homework on researching the company.

Sources of Information

The Company

One of the very best sources of information is the company itself. Many larger companies have a public relations department that can get you an annual report and marketing pieces, and they can also show you where to find articles on the company or its employees. If you have arranged an interview, ask for the job description of the position you are interviewing for.

The Library

College and public libraries are great places to start your research. You'll find periodical indexes especially useful in finding articles about companies and individuals. As your research gets more so-phisticated, however, you should realize that not all libraries are equal in their capacity to support good research on businesses. You may need to make a few phone calls to find out which libraries in your area will best serve your needs. Talk to reference librarians, especially those who specialize in business. They'll be happy to direct you to the information you need.

The Internet

The Internet has become a quick and convenient resource for re-search. You can do a search on a company's or an individual's name and be directed to quite a bit of information. We offer two cau-tions, however:

> 1. Not all information on the Internet is accurate! You can't be sure who posted something on a Web page, or where they got their facts. Always double-check the information before accepting it as true.

> 2. Don't substitute the Internet for the library! Let the Internet supplement your library research. Many of the top business research sites charge you for access and much of this information is accessible at the library.

A Picture is Worth a Job!

We got this note from a candidate who won the job—

"I was interviewing with Procter and Gamble, the largest consumer products company in the country. I really wanted the job, so I went out to a number of grocery stores and took pictures of where and how their products were being displayed. I also gathered some information on merchandising and placement of products. I talked to a couple of store managers and learned a lot from them. I got a good sense of what merchandising in the chains was all about.

"So—when I went into my interview, I opened my briefcase and took out my pictures to demonstrate that I had studied the displays at different stores, and could show that the company was better represented in some stores than in others. My homework, and especially the pictures, gave me something that would set me apart from the pack. I was the only one who did it!

"The recruiter offered me the job. He told me I got the job because of my creative research. It didn't take much time or effort, but that little extra difference made me shine above the rest!"

12

Building Your Job Network

"Networking" is just a fancy term for developing a list of people who can help you in your career. Whenever you meet someone and tell him about your experience, your capabilities, or your ambitions, you've added another person to your network. Whenever you ask a former teacher or employer to give you a reference, you're contacting someone who is part of the network you already have. In reality, we're all networking, all the time. This chapter gives you a systematic way to go about it.

Your Own Personal Business Card

As you begin your job search, you should develop and have printed your own personal business card. Business cards are collected by most business professionals. Though someone may throw away or misplace your résumé, they will most likely tuck your business card away for future reference. A personal business card can simply contain your name, address, phone number, e-mail address, and possibly the title or type of position you are seeking.

Networking is the most effective way to find good job opportunities. Sixty-five percent of job opportunities are never listed in the want ads, posted on the Internet, or sent to job recruiters! And yet those positions are filled—by people who have learned about those jobs through their network. As your network grows, more and more people will become aware of your qualifications and career goals. When a job opens up that would be a good fit for you, a strong network will increase the chances that someone will contact you about that opening. They might even refer you directly to the person who has the power to hire you!

The Network Planning Worksheet

The **Networking Planning Worksheet** (Form 5) will help you develop an organized method for networking with people who can help you. The worksheet will help you to keep track of your contacts and to uncover as many new contacts as possible. Your networking efforts, used in conjunction with informational interviews, will make sure that you're able to talk to the people who can help you most!

When you make contact with someone, you should have the following goals in mind:

❖ Find out information about a career, industry, company, competitor, or customer.

❖ Let people know that you're in a job search and what you're looking for. Always send or leave them your résumé and business card

❖ Get the names of others who can help you.

At the end of every contact, you should have accomplished all three goals. If you follow this procedure, you'll be able to greatly expand your job search and have more people looking out for the right opportunity for you.

Getting Started

Your first step will be to create a list of at least 20 names of people you can begin networking with. Who do you put on the list? Basically, anyone you respect and whose judgment and guidance you value. At this point, you're not in a position to zero in on a specific company. Your list might start with former teachers and employers, colleagues, former co-workers, and people you know in a non-business context. *(Be sure to make at least 50 copies of the Network Planning Worksheet before you begin.)* Complete the top portion of a Network Planning Worksheet for each person on your list, and then make a brief list of questions that you want to ask this person. Again, at the beginning of this process, you're not targeting a specific company, so your questions will be more general. As your network grows through references, your job search will become more focused.

> In order to succeed, you must know what you are doing, like what you are doing, and believe in what you are doing.
>
> *- Will Rogers*

Also determine whether you want to interview this person by phone or in person. The more power and influence a person has, the greater the effort you should make to meet with him in person, but because of this person's status, it may be very difficult to arrange a meeting. Be ready to settle for a telephone interview. In some situations, you'll be able to interview the person on the first call. At other times, you will need to schedule a time to follow up with him to conduct the interview.

Your next step is to begin calling each person. Below is a sample introduction for your phone calls:

> "Hi, this is _____, and I'm calling you because I'm in the middle of a job search and I could use some advice! I'm contacting you specifically because [*state reason you believe this person can offer you advice*]. Might I have a few moments of your time to ask you a few questions?"

If the person has time to talk, then dive right into your questions! Be sure to have each question ready, as well as your pen and paper. Be sensitive to the amount of time the person is able to give you, especially if you're calling during work hours. If you're not able to complete the interview, ask for some additional time or ask for a convenient time to call back.

Before concluding your call, **be sure to ask the person if there are other people that he could direct you to for additional help and information.** <u>ALWAYS ASK FOR ANOTHER REFER-RAL!</u> Note that the Network Planning Worksheet has space for three names. By all means, try to get more than one name—this is how you build your network! Be sure to get the names and phone numbers accurately. Ask the person if you can use his name when you call the new referral. If the person asks you *not* to use his or her name, it is extremely important to respect that request! You must not reveal the person's name or the method by which you received your new referral's name. If you are given permission to use that person's name, be sure that you do. This will give you more credibility and a better opportunity to get the information you want.

Every time you add a new name, be sure to complete a Network Planning Worksheet for that person. This way, you'll never lose a contact, and you'll be able to better manage your contacts. We suggest that you keep your networking sheets in a separate three-ring binder, but you could keep the contacts in the back of your **PoP Portfolio.**

To conclude the phone call, briefly summarize the main things you learned and thank your contact for his or her time. Note the date of your interview—this can help you as you review your job campaign. You'll want to refer to the last time you spoke if you need to contact that person again. Be sure to send a brief thank-you card stating your appreciation for the help you received. This can be faxed or mailed immediately after your interview. *(You'll find more on thank-you notes in Chapter 15.)*

Telephone Skills

No doubt you've figured out that most of your networking conversations, and virtually all of your initial contacts, are done over the telephone. Most of the initial contacts you make for formal job interviews are also done by phone, so **it's essential that your telephone skills are first-rate.**

Many people don't realize how important the first phone call to a company can be. Professional recruiters, who deal with hundreds of job-seekers, say that they're constantly amazed at the poor communications skills and ignorance of professional phone etiquette demonstrated by many candidates. Here are some basic rules to follow:

> ❖ **Treat every person you speak to as if he or she were the person doing the hiring.** Sometimes the person answering the phone actually is the hiring manager! Just as important, a receptionist or administrative assistant may be giving feedback — solicited or unsolicited — to the hiring manager about job candidates. Treat just one person with disrespect, and that person could wreck your chance to get an interview.

❖ **Speak clearly, concisely, and professionally.** Identify yourself and the purpose of your call clearly. Be polite and courteous.

❖ **Speak with energy and enthusiasm.** You don't want to sound like a carnival barker, but a lifeless phone delivery won't create the positive impression you want to leave with the person on the other end of the line.

❖ **Listen closely to how people identify themselves on the phone and address them that way.** If someone answers the phone, "This is Mr. Long," for example, address him as Mr. Long, even if you know his first name. If he says, "This is Bob Long," you should probably still say "Mr. Long," unless he asks you to use his first name.

❖ **Never use slang terms or pet names** like "Buddy," "Pal," "Friend," "Honey," "Dear," "Dude," and so on.

❖ **Always have a pen, paper, and your portfolio handy when making phone calls.** Be prepared to write down the names of people you talk with, their phone numbers, addresses, and so on. You will appear unprepared if you have to ask the person to hold on while you get a pen and paper.

❖ **Find a quiet place to make your phone calls.** Don't have the TV, stereo, or other distracting noises in the background. Locate yourself where other family members or roommates can't be heard by the person receiving your phone call.

❖ **Use a quality phone** that sounds good to the person on the other end of the line. Avoid wireless phones, either cordless units or cellular phones, if they tend to cut out or produce a lot of static.

If You Speak with an Accent

If English isn't your first language, don't be discouraged in your career quest! Our great country was built in very large measure by immigrant people, most of whom weren't native English speakers, and their contribution to our society was, and continues to be, tremendous. You have a great deal to offer, and we're sure you'll find rewarding employment using your **PoP Portfolio.**

Nevertheless, when talking on the telephone, you lose the eye contact, gesture, and other visual cues to assist in communication, so clear telephone speaking is an absolute must. Practice with your tape recorder and with your friends to develop clarity over the phone.

Much the same goes for people seeking work in a new section of the country. A Chicagoan may have trouble being understood in Atlanta, and a Southern accent may be hard for a Yankee to understand. At no time do we advise you to speak in a way that's forced or artificial for you, but you should practice to be sure you're clearly understood.

Improving Your Phone Delivery

Right now, how would you rate your phone skills? Excellent? Pretty good? Only fair? Or are you not sure exactly how you come across on the phone? It's amazing how "flat" most people sound on the phone! They may be relating important information, but their voices lack energy and enthusiasm, and they fail to articulate the information clearly and concisely. This happens because most people have never listened to themselves and how they communicate.

Phone Skills Make or Break Your Initial Contact

With over 20-plus years of recruiting and literally conducting thousands and thousands of phone interviews, I would say that only 10-20% of candidates have good phone skills. Guess who I bring in for formal interviews? All of the client companies I recruit for demand candidates with excellent communication skills...and this begins with the ability to communicate over the phone effectively.

-Rick Nelles

One of the best tools to help you diagnose your weaknesses and improve your telephone skills is a small tape recorder. (*We recommend getting a little "micro-cassette" recorder. You'll find it useful in lots of ways.*) There are two ways that you can use the tape recorder to monitor and improve your skills:.

1. Rehearse your phone calls with the tape recorder. Have someone role-play with you or simply practice your phone delivery by yourself.

2. Have the tape recorder in front of you as you make some actual phone calls.

After taping yourself, listen to the tapes and ask yourself these questions:

❖ Is my speech easy to understand?

❖ Do I sound enthusiastic and energetic?

❖ Is my delivery clear and concise?

Have other people listen to the tape and get their feedback. Ask them the same three questions you asked yourself. Take their advice to heart as to how you can improve your energy, enthusiasm, and clarity.

Constant improvement of your telephone skills as you build your network and conduct your informational interviews will help you immensely as you work toward the formal interview that gets you the job!

13

The Power of Informational Interviewing

The informational interview is the most underutilized tool in career transition. It's valuable whether you're just starting out or shifting to a new career. Informational interviewing serves many crucial purposes, but most people don't take the time to gather the information that will help them make sound career choices, network effectively, and get better prepared for the formal interview.

Informational interviewing is a must before entering the formal interviewing process. A failure to understand the difference between the informational interview and the formal interview is one of the biggest mistakes people make in the interviewing process. Many people fail in the formal interview when they enter it with an informational interviewing mind-set. The best way to cure this problem is to understand the differences between the two and to approach each in the proper way.

In an Informational Interview:

❖ You are NOT being screened against other candidates.

❖ You are NOT discussing a specific job opportunity.

❖ You are gathering information about a career, an industry, or a specific company.

❖ You are networking with people who can help you learn about job openings and gain access to hiring managers.

❖ Your goal is to gather information that can help you in the formal interview.

In a Formal Interview:

❖ You are competing against other candidates for a job.

❖ You are discussing a specific job opening or potential opening.

❖ Your goal is to get the job offer.

Hiring managers don't want their time wasted by candidates who are treating the formal interview as an informational interview. It's dishonest of you to make an appointment for a formal interview when you're really just looking around. In the formal interview they want performance—it's showtime for you!

People may also become irritated if you tell them you're coming in for an informational interview and then you start hustling for a job offer. However, you should be aware that there are situations where the informational interview can *become* a formal interview. If you arrange an informational interview with someone who also has the power to hire, you need to be ready to shift into a formal interview mode if that person indicates that there may be opportunities available for you at his company.

Benefits of Informational Interviews

As we said, informational interviewing is one of the most powerful tools you have to succeed in career transition. Amazingly, a majority of people overlook this golden opportunity. There are many benefits to informational interviewing.

Make Better Career Choices

Informational interviews allow you to get firsthand knowledge about the careers or jobs you're considering. Research is very important, but just reading about careers only gives you half the story. You'll get more insights into a career by talking to people who have walked along that path. You'll hear their emotions and attitudes and you'll learn exactly what it takes to be successful!

**People Hire People Who Communicate
Most Like Themselves**

Every sales seminar will tell you how important it is to become a "chameleon" when selling. The ability for you to adapt your communication style to another person is an ability that will take you far.

There are many books on identifying personality and communication styles and how to adapt your style to someone else's. The DiSC® *(see page 55)* can give you insight into your own communication style and also teach you about the communication styles of other people.

Informational interviews will give you very valuable practice in assessing your subject's communication style, so that in your formal interview, you'll be able "read" the hiring manager and adjust your presentation for maximum impact!

Identify the Best Companies and Avoid Bad Ones

Through informational interviews, you can learn which companies treat their employees well, offer superior products or services, and have the brightest futures. There are many bad companies that try to hire good people, and their recruiters will try to sell you on the company. Informational interviews with former employees, competitors, and customers will help you avoid companies that treat their employees badly or have notoriously high turnover rates.

Network to Uncover New Opportunities

Informational interviewing is absolutely the best networking tool! Informational interviews give the person time to get to know you and your career goals. They'll remember you when they come across one of those unlisted job opportunities that's right for you.

Reduce "Job Hopping"

There are two major situations that contribute to job hopping: going to work for a bad company and taking a job based on misconceptions about a career. Informational interviews help you avoid both pitfalls.

Identify Needs for the Formal Interview

When you have a good understanding of the needs of the position, you'll be able to go into the interview better prepared. The hiring manager will be impressed that you've done your homework and will appreciate someone coming into the interview with a strong understanding of the position. (*See Chapter 15 for more on identifying needs.*)

Gain Insights into the Hiring Manager

Many times you'll be able to do informational interviews with people who know the person who will interview you for a job. Understanding the hiring manager's personality, communication style, passions, dislikes, and personal interests will help you customize your presentation to that person.

Practice Intervew Skills

Informational interviews allow you the opportunity to practice communication skills. Do not treat informational interviews as "informal" interviews! Any time you're interviewing someone in relation to your job search or preparation, you should act like a professional. At the end of informational interviews, it's wise to get feedback from the person you were interviewing about your communication skills.

Ask Better Questions in Interviews

In almost every formal interviewing situation, you have an opportunity to ask questions. Informational interviews give you lots of material from which you can frame pertinent questions, and the knowledge you gain in informational interviews gives you the ability to talk with the hiring manager on a more intelligent level. The hiring manager will appreciate talking with someone who understands the industry, the company, its competitors, and customers.

Types of Informational Interviews

In this section, we'll break down informational interviews into five categories. It's important to realize that these categories are very artificial and that almost every informational interview you conduct will have aspects of all five categories. We're breaking them down into categories so that you can see the enormous amount of information you'll be able to get through informational interviews.

There are five basic types of information to gather:

❖ Career information

❖ Industry information

❖ Company information

❖ Competitor information

❖ Customer information

Every informational interview will help you gather information about these areas. Certain interviews will focus on different areas, though. For example, early in your informational interviewing, you'll likely focus on career and industry information, as you're deciding what career you want to pursue and in what industry you'd like to work. Once you decide on a career and an industry, you'll begin to focus more on specific companies, their competitors, and their customers as you begin preparing for formal interviews.

Career Information

As you begin deciding which career you want to pursue, most of your informational interviews will focus on gathering career information, to help you make wise career choices. By truly understanding the career you are pursuing, you'll also be better able to create realistic goals. **Your main objective is to determine whether or not the career you're investigating is the right career for your future.**

Avoid Rude Surprises: Learn About the Job

"Most students say that they've chosen their field because they like the kind of work it involves....so, in most cases, employers are starting out with new hires who at least like the idea of what their job entails. But that's where the disconnect may begin. As one employer noted, the challenge is to have the student's idea of the job he/she has been hired for match the actual job....First-year work that involves learning the ropes instead of star-caliber assignments is likely to disappoint."

-Job Outlook '99

Many people launch headlong into a career without first seriously investigating what that career entails, never truly understanding what that career is all about! A year or two on the job, and they realize that they've made a bad career selection. Career-related informational interviewing will help you make wise choices, so you'll enjoy much greater career satisfaction.

During these interviews, you'll probably learn a lot of information that fits into the other areas. Be sure to keep track of this information, because it could be very helpful later on! The bulk of the information you seek in a career-related informational interview, however, should focus on the following:

❖ What is a typical day or work-week like? What type of activities will I be doing?

❖ What three things are necessary to be successful in this career?

❖ What type of educational background does it take to be successful in this career?

❖ What type of experience does it take to be successful in this career?

❖ What job skills do I need to be successful in this career?

❖ What type of personality does it take to be successful in this career?

❖ What kind of future will I have in this career?

❖ What type of entry-level income can I expect to make?

❖ What type of income can I expect to make in future years (three, five, ten years down the road)?

❖ What are the downsides of this career?

It will be helpful to talk to people at all levels in your chosen career. For example, if you are considering a career as an accountant, you will want to talk to people who are just starting a career in accounting, people three to five years into their career, and people who have had a long, successful career in accounting. You will also want to talk to people at different size companies and in different industries.

How to Stop Finishing as Runner-Up

How LeRoy turned things around:

I was so tired of coming in second, I could scream! I was getting job interviews with no problem, and was easily moving on to second and third interviews. But I was always coming in second and losing the job to someone else! So my brother arranged for me to meet with a friend of his who is a professional recruiter. He told me, "LeRoy, I can see why you're getting those second interviews. You've got good communication skills and a great track record. But what you need is a knockout punch. You've got to go into that interview with some proof of performance that'll make you stand out from the crowd."

The recruiter told me to call on four or five of the major buyers that dealt with the company I was going to interview with. From the buyers, he told me to get the names of sales people that call on them from different companies. So I met with some of the sales reps, and I asked one of them if I could ride with him for half a day. I learned a lot and really felt prepared for my interview.

However, the hiring manager was a real S.O.B. He liked to intimidate people—that was his way of seeing what they were made of. He took a look at my résumé and threw it back across the desk. He said, "Why are you here today? I don't see anything on your résumé that makes me interested in you." I told him I really wanted to work for his company, at which point he went ballistic. "That's the poorest answer I've ever heard! You don't know anything about us, so how can you sit there and say you want to work for our company?"

I pulled out some information from my briefcase and explained that I had interviewed several of his buyers and competitors. I handed him the information and said, "Here are some notes of what people are saying about your company. By the way, I hope you don't mind, but I also rode with one of your sales reps for half a day." The hiring manager was stunned.

Never in the history of the company had they ever made a job offer on the first interview, but I got an offer on the spot! I'd been coming in second all the time, but my homework was the knockout punch I needed to break a company record before I was even hired!

How many people should you talk to? As many as you can! As long as you're moving ahead in your career transition, you should continue to hold informational interviews with people in your chosen career. This will help you to continue networking until you find the right job.

The information that you gather from career interviews can be used in the formal interview process. If you're asked why you are pursuing a specific position, you can share with the hiring manager the research you've done on that career and the reasons you want to pursue that career. You should also incorporate this material in your Proactive Career Goals worksheet.

Industry Information

As you are interviewing people about their careers, you should also be gathering information about specific industries. After you choose a career, you'll discover a wide range of industries in which you can exercise that career choice. Informational interviews will help you **identify industries that you are interested in.** In the interviews, you'll be asking questions like these:

❖ What do you like about your industry?

❖ What do you dislike about your industry?

❖ What type of future does this industry have?

❖ What are the greatest challenges facing this industry?

❖ What are the best companies in this industry?

❖ What are some of the least respected companies in this industry?

The industry information that you gather will also be valuable during your formal interviews. As you talk with hiring managers, you'll be able to discuss the industry on a very professional level. You'll be able to share insights about the future of the industry and ask questions about the challenges you uncovered in the informational interviews.

> For six months now, I've been visiting the workplaces of America, administering a simple test. I call it the "pronoun test." I ask frontline workers a few general questions about the company. If the answers I get back describe the company in terms like "they" and "them," then I know it's one kind of company. If the answers are put in terms like "we" or "us," I know it's a different kind of company.
>
> *-Robert B. Reich, Former Secretary of Labor*

Company Information

In all of your interviews, you'll be getting information about specific companies. Sometimes you'll learn a lot about a company before you know whether or not you'll be interviewing there. At some point, though, you'll have identified a company that you think you might like to work for. You may even have scheduled an interview there. Then you'll want to focus your informational interviews on specific information about that company. Some questions you may want to ask will include:

❖ Where does this company stand in comparison to others in the industry?

❖ How strong is the company financially?

❖ What is this company's reputation?

❖ What is this company's market share?

❖ Who are this company's three toughest competitors?

❖ What is this company's mission statement?

❖ What are the strengths of this company?

❖ What are the weaknesses of this company?

❖ Where do you see this company going in the future?

❖ What are the benefits of working for this company?

❖ What type of employees does this company hire?

❖ Does this company have a reputation for high turnover?

❖ Does this company treat its employees well?

❖ How would you describe the corporate culture?

❖ How many employees work at this company?

❖ Is it privately held or is it a public company?

❖ Which stock market lists this company?

❖ Do you know anyone at another company in the industry?

These questions are meant to help you be sure that you won't go to work for a bad company, or even interview with one! There are many "toxic" companies out there, trying to hire good people, and you'll hear many "horror stories." The company will put on a great show to get you hired, but once you begin working there, it's a whole different ballgame! Informational interviewing can definitely help you avoid bad companies, because you won't get this kind of information at the library or off the Internet — you'll only get it by talking to people.

Information you learn about a company can be very powerful in several areas of your interview. First, your insights into the company will be very interesting to the hiring manager. You can also explain to the hiring manager why you want to work for his company instead of someone else's—and not just because this company pays more or has better benefits. Finally, you can demonstrate solid knowledge about the strengths of the company, its future, and its superiority over competitors.

Competitor Information

Some of the best information about a company is held by its competition. **You can gain a lot of information about a company by interviewing people working for its chief competitors.** Much of the time, the competitive information that you get will come from interviewing people for industry information. Here are some general questions that you can ask to get the information that you want:

❖ Who are your toughest competitors?

❖ What are the strengths of [a competitor]?

❖ What are the weaknesses of [a competitor]?

❖ Who are some of the least respected companies in your industry?

❖ What are some of the best companies to work for in your industry?

❖ Are there any companies that you would stay away from?

❖ Do you know any companies who have a bad reputation for the way they treat employees?

This information can be beneficial when discussing the positive or negative aspects of the company you are interviewing with. You can simply tell the hiring manager about the insights you gathered while talking to competitors. Hiring managers will find this information interesting, and they'll be impressed that you made the effort to gather it. Better yet, record the information in an organized way and leave it with the hiring manager! They'll be excited to see information about customers and competitors that has been uncovered through direct interviews. This will show that you're a person who can get "the inside scoop."

Customer Information

A good source of information is to talk to the customers or potential customers of the companies you want to interview with. These informational interviews can produce some very interesting results, and this information will be especially helpful to you if you want to work in upper-level management, sales, marketing, or customer service. Here are some questions you will want to ask customers:

❖ Who are the best companies you work with?

❖ Who are the best representatives [use whatever position is most appropriate for your desired job] that you work with?

❖ Why do you do business with Company X?

❖ Why don't you do business with Company X?

❖ What would Company X have to do to get your business?

❖ If you could change one thing about Company X, what would it be?

❖ If you don't do business with Company X, why do you use Company Y?

In "The Informational Interview in Action" (*see below*), Carol knew how important it is for a salesperson to understand the needs of the customer and the customer's perception of the company. She knew that the hiring manager would find the customer's comments interesting, and she used the customer's information to get his attention. She also used the information to show the hiring manager that there was a need in the market that he might not have identified, and she showed how she would be able to meet that need.

You can also use customer information as an incentive to get the hiring manager to meet with you. You can tell him that you've been talking with customers and have uncovered some interesting information that they might find very valuable. Set up a meeting to share this information and you'll have established an important contact that may lead to a job!

**How the Informational Interview Helped Carol
Tap the Hidden Job Market and Get the Job**

Carol was one of the most successful and creative candidates that we have encountered. She had four job offers on the table and had contacted us to see what she could learn about the companies. She had already talked to others and had exhausted her library search for information. We were very impressed with the number of offers she had received, so we asked her how she achieved such success.

First, she knew what she wanted. She had decided to pursue a sales career, and she zeroed in on the industry in which she wanted to work. After she identified the industry, which was the food industry, she began to network like crazy. She went to grocery stores and talked to salespeople while they were working the shelves, getting ready for their sales calls. She would walk up, introduce herself, and ask, "Can you help me out and give me some advice? I want to be a salesperson like you, but I need some information. Could I ask you a couple questions?" She told us that every salesperson she talked to was unbelievably helpful. She then went down her question sheet:

❖ What do you like about your job and company?

❖ What don't you like about your job and company?

❖ What are three key job skills you must have to be good at what you do?

❖ What is the most challenging problem in your industry right now?

❖ Who are the best companies to work for in your industry? Why?

❖ What companies should I stay away from?

❖ Would you share the names of other sales reps?

❖ What companies do they work for?

❖ Who is the person you sell to at this store?

❖ Who is your favorite buyer? What store do they work for?

Her next step was to contact buyers at the store level. Her approach to buyers was similar to her approach to the sales reps. She would introduce herself and let them know that she needed some advice. She would then ask if they could take a few moments to answer a few questions. Some of the questions she asked are listed below:

❖ What do you think it takes to be a good sales rep?

❖ Out of all the salespeople who call on you, who is the best and why? Whom do they work for?

❖ What is your biggest pet peeve about salespeople?

❖ What major changes do you see happening in your industry?

❖ Who is the headquarters buyer for your company? (*This was important because the headquarters buyers were the people Carol wanted to contact in order to get the names of hiring managers.)*

Carol said all the buyers that she talked to were extremely helpful. Her next step was to contact headquarters buyers (who manage the store buyers) to set up informational interviews with them. She knew that they would have contacts with the top sales reps in most companies.

After she had all her information put together, she called hiring sales managers. She only called on the good companies that she had uncovered in her research.

When she called, her script went something like this:

"Mr./Ms. sales manager, I was given your name by several of your customers. They [name a few of the buyers] had a lot of good things to say about you. I also talked to some of your competitors and they said some pretty interesting things about your company. If you grant me just ten minutes of your time, I would like to share this information with you. I am looking for a sales position in your industry and I would like to find out what it takes to be a salesperson in your organization."

After meeting with several hiring sales managers, one of the hiring sales managers called her back. At the time she had talked to him, he did not have an opening. He informed her that he had been putting off firing a rep because of the hassle of finding a better salesperson to hire in place of that rep. After meeting Carol and seeing her initiative and the efforts she had put forth in finding a new position, the sales manager was now able to fire the failing rep and offer Carol the job.

Carol's success would not have occurred if she had not taken the initiative to go out and conduct informational interviews. The best job seekers find ways to find the job they want.

14

Preparing for the
Formal Interview

As we mentioned in Chapter 11, there are several things you'll be doing while you assemble your **Proof of Performance Portfolio:** researching, building your network, improving your phone skills, conducting informational interviews, and so on. All these activities help to prepare you for your eventual formal job interview. In this chapter, we'll talk about some exercises you can do that are geared specifically toward the formal interview.

> Success comes when preparation meets opportunity.
>
> *-Unknown*

Most of the information here is not unique to this book. There are many fine books available on effective interviewing, and we encourage you to look at some of them to make sure you know the basics. The reason we've included these exercises is because **we have personally observed that very few people actually practice these skills.** Preparing a great portfolio and not working on your interviewing is like getting the finest cookware money can buy and never preparing a meal.

Quality equipment will help, but it will not make you an expert unless you practice your skills.

Interview Skills

Your ability to communicate with impact in an interview situation is an essential key to setting yourself apart from your competition. You must commit to becoming the best you can be in the interview process, and to do that, you must perfect your skills through many types of practice.   Here are some proven methods for improving your speaking and interviewing skills.

The Campus Career Center: A Valuable Resource

"There seems to be a trend...among employers, toward strengthening their links to colleges...A number of organizations found themselves paying the price for having dismantled their college relations and recruitment programs when their college hiring needs were down...Some said that they are trying to have a stronger presence on campus, to become more involved with campus and student organizations, and to build their campus relationships."

- Job Outlook '99

Working with a Coach

One of the absolute best ways to improve any kind of communication skill is to work one-on-one with a person who can give you feedback and make suggestions for improvement — in short, someone to act as your coach. And **you should make every effort to work with a professional.** It's really impossible to know your skill level until you've been critiqued by a pro. Friends are fine to practice with, but many times they have no idea how the best interviewers perform. Here are some ways to find a coach:

❖ If you're a college student, you have an excellent resource at your disposal. Your school's career planning and placement office probably offers services to help you improve your job interviewing skills. If it does, be sure to take advantage of this service. They can put you in touch with someone who can give you a professional critique. (*You may not need to be a current student to use this service. Many schools also allow their alumni to use their career and placement services, so definitely check it out.*)

❖ As you conduct your informational interviews, be sure to ask for a critique of your interpersonal communication skills! This doubles the value of your informational interviews: you're getting valuable career information and building your interviewing skills at the same time. You may come across someone who would be an excellent coach as you conduct informational interviews.

❖ Seek out someone, preferably a professional who has hired a lot of people, to coach or mentor you through your career transition. After you identify this person, approach him by saying, "I need a coach to help me become the best I can be at communicating who I am and what I can do for a company." You'll be amazed at how many people will be honored when you ask them for help! Think of times when others have asked you for help and how flattered you were. If you could help them, you helped them, didn't you? Successful people give back. Attempt to find someone who is well networked and who will push and motivate you during your training. And don't be surprised if this person becomes a lifelong friend!

Rehearsing with a Tape Recorder

Using a tape recorder to practice your responses to interview questions is invaluable. By practicing your responses, you will be able to better articulate your stories to the hiring manager and do so with energy and enthusiasm. This also has the added benefit of being something you can do anytime by yourself. Keep your little microcassette recorder with you all the time, and you can practice whenever you have a few spare moments — in the car, on a walk, anytime.

Additional Help

For more about interviewing skills and questions we suggest you pick up *Interview Power: Selling Yourself Face To Face* by Tom Washington. It is an easy-to-read yet comprehensive book on how to sell yourself in an interview. It includes additional lists of questions to help you prepare for the interview.

Here is a list of several of the most-often asked questions in job interviews. Take this list and rehearse your answers into a tape recorder. You may even want to write some of your answers out. Tape your answers and then listen to the responses.

❖ What is your greatest strength?

❖ What is your greatest weakness?

❖ What are your top career accomplishments?

❖ What are your career goals?

❖ Tell me about your last job?

After taping your responses, ask yourself these questions as you do a self-critique:

❖ Does my response actually answer the question?

❖ Do I sound confident and enthusiastic in my response?

❖ Does my response identify the hiring manager's need and how I can meet that need? (*More on "identifying needs" later in this chapter.*)

❖ Is my speech free of "you know," "like," "uh," and other distracting phrases that will appear unprofessional to a hiring manager?

Continually practice with the handheld tape recorder. Practice answering any questions that you believe will be asked in the interview process. Save your tapes from your early practice sessions and compare them with tapes made even two or three weeks later. You'll be amazed at your improvement.

Using Video to Tell the Whole Story

As good as rehearsing with an audio tape recorder is, using video-tape is an even stronger medium for perfecting your interview and communication skills. Most people now have access to videotape equipment. If at all possible, have someone who is experienced at hiring professionals interview you on videotape. If you do not have access to someone with that experience, try to get someone who will take your efforts seriously. When watching yourself respond to interview questions on videotape, watch for the following:

❖ Body language *(If you are not familiar with body language, there are many books that can help you.)*

❖ Posture

❖ Facial expressions

❖ Nervous habits (both verbal and physical)

❖ Eye contact

❖ Voice projection

❖ Listening skills

Practice using your **PoP Portfolio** in the interview (*more on using your portfolio in the next chapter*). It will take some time to get adept at using the portfolio smoothly.

The Power of Videotape

Golf is a passion of mine and I will never forget the first time I saw my swing on videotape. I had no idea I was doing a lot of the things I was doing! Seeing my swing helped me get a better handle on where I was and where I wanted to go.

Videotape has the power to show you where you're making mistakes. Why do you think so many companies have their sales reps videotaped giving a presentation? You've got it: It teaches them how to sell better. Interviewing is selling!

- Rick Nelles

Role-Playing

Role-playing is one of the most powerful training tools available to you. It's as close as you can come to the real interview. Work with your coach or someone else who has interviewing experience, and provide them with a list of questions. Have them ask you the questions along with any follow-up questions they believe are appropriate. Try to create an environment that resembles a real interview. During the initial role-plays, stop often to re-view specific responses. The interviewer should evaluate your responses by considering these questions:

❖ Do your responses answer the question?

❖ Do you give specific examples of past performance?

❖ Was the answer clear and concise?

❖ Do you have any habits that are annoying or dis-concerting for the interviewer?

Next, you should practice an entire interview without stop-ping. This is important to develop endurance. Interviewing can be rigorous and you need rigorous preparation. Take this practice seriously. Try to simulate a real interview as much as you can. Sports teams begin each season with exhibition games and theatri-cal productions play to preview audiences before the official open-ing. In both cases, they're trying to get fully prepared for when it really counts. You need to do the same in your preparation for the formal interview.

Identifying Needs

An often-overlooked skill to develop is the ability to "identify needs." Every hiring manager has a written or mental list of what he needs in a candidate to fill the position. Your goal is to **identify as many of these needs as possible and to prove to the interviewer that you meet these needs.** That's the enormous advantage your **Proof of Performance Portfolio** gives you: a concrete way to document your ability to meet their needs. You can uncover needs in several ways:

Research

As you research careers, you'll be able to identify some relatively generic needs. For example, if you do your research about sales representative positions, you will learn that cold-calling skills are almost always important. If that's the case, then you want to have some kind of documentation that you're able to conduct cold calls and prospect for accounts.

Informal Interviews

As you talk to individuals who work for specific companies, you should be able to identify a corporate culture and what type of people fit into that culture. For example, suppose you're seeking a position as an accountant at a medium-sized accounting firm. You find out through your interviews that the company likes candidates with at least a 3.5 GPA and an extroverted personality. If you fit that description, you'll want to have your grades ready and have documentation that you are an outgoing "people" person.

Job Description

If you're able to get a job description before the interview, this will help you tremendously with identifying the basic needs of the position. To receive one, simply ask the hiring manager or his assistant if there is a job description available and if you can have a copy.

Formal Interview

Throughout the entire interview, you'll want to listen for cues from the hiring manager on what he is looking for. This is where you'll need to be able to think on your feet. Always have your notepad open and write down the needs you hear expressed by the hiring manager. You may not be able to address them at that moment, but you'll want to make sure you don't forget to address them before the end of the interview.

We have created a Needs Worksheet (Form 6) for you to use in preparation for the interview and to take into the interview. You'll want to record all the needs you uncovered in preparation for the interview. Next to the need you should write some brief notes of how you meet that need and any documentation that you can use to help make your point.

Understanding needs and being able to address them will put you way ahead of your competition. It will also prepare you to close the interview effectively and increase your chances of winning the position.

15

Using Your PoP Portfolio
in the Interview

In this chapter, we'll address the final step in your job search campaign: the formal interview and how you use your **Proof of Performance Portfolio** to make a strong impression on the hiring manager. **By this point, you should be fully prepared for this experience**—you've practiced your phone and interviewing skills, and you've assimilated extensive information about the company through your research and informational interviewing. And, of course, your portfolio is in order, giving you an edge over all other candidates for the position!

One important piece of equipment we suggest that you **carry into your interview is a briefcase.** Pick any style that suits you, but be sure it looks businesslike, not cute or "sporty." Inside, you should have extra business cards, a notepad, a day planner, and thank-you cards, all neatly arranged. You should also have your **Proof of Performance Portfolio** arranged so that when you open your briefcase it will be easy to see.

You want your briefcase to appear organized because it will be the first indication the hiring manager will get of your personal organization skills. If you don't have a briefcase, we definitely encourage you to purchase one. If you're unable to purchase a briefcase or for some reason you'd prefer not to use one, simply carry your **PoP Portfolio** and notepad into the interview under your arm. Be sure that they're in your left arm, because you want to have your right hand free to shake hands with the hiring manager!

Entering the Interview

A few years back, there was a TV commercial for a personal grooming product, and the slogan they used was, "You never get a second chance to make a first impression." That's absolutely true—**the first impression you make on the hiring manager can be the most important moment of the interview.** Upon entering the office, extend your right hand confidently to the hiring manager and introduce yourself, using your first and last names. Speak in a strong voice, have a firm handshake, make eye contact with the hiring manager, and smile.

Make A Good First Impression—Fast!

"According to a survey by Accountemps...it takes an average of 16 minutes for hiring managers to tell if the candidate is a good match. 'Candidates need to be ready to answer questions that are likely to come up at the beginning of the meetings,' says Max Messmer, chairman of Accountemps. These questions include queries about themselves, why they're planning to leave their current job and their experience. Answers

> should be delivered in a concise, poised and enthusiastic manner. 'During the initial minutes of an interview, managers will be assessing whether candidates should move to the next step in the hiring process.'"
>
> *- National Business Employment Weekly*

Throughout this book we've been referring to "the hiring manager." We've used this rather nebulous term because you might be interviewed by almost anyone, depending on the company. "Hiring manager" simply means the person with the power to hire you. At a large corporation, you're likely to encounter a human resources specialist, whose only job is to screen candidates, and who might have limited knowledge of the specific job you're applying for. At a small, family-owned company, you're likely to be interviewing with the founder, president, chief financial officer, and head truck driver—and that's all the same person! In all cases, however, **a very important interviewing skill is the ability to immediately establish rapport with the hiring manager.**

Rapport is simply a personal connection, a harmonious relationship. You may already have learned a few personal things about the hiring manager in your informational interviewing, and you'll be prepared to mention those things. But even if you know nothing in advance about the hiring manager, you can still establish rapport. Simply look around the room and find something that you're able to comment on. Look for the things that are prominently displayed in the office: pictures, trophies, diplomas, certificates, books, or anything else the hiring manager obviously enjoys or is proud of. (For example, we have many pictures of golf courses hanging on the walls of our offices. This is a sure sign to anyone entering our office that golf is an open topic of conversation.) Select something that relates to your own life; perhaps there's a travel picture of a place you've visited, or a trophy from a sport you've played, or a diploma from the same college you attended. This opening "small talk" is not frivolous — hiring managers like to find people who can zero in on the interests and needs of others, and your ability to establish rapport also shows that you can think on your feet. You're not trying to become close pals with the hiring manager, but breaking the ice like this can set the stage for a comfortable business conversation.

After this initial time of establishing rapport, ask the hiring manager if you can give him a clean copy of your résumé. You'll have put your résumés in the front pocket of the portfolio binder, so this will give you the opportunity **get your Proof of Performance Portfolio out.** As you take out your portfolio, do so in a subtle way that allows the hiring manager to see the cover. The uniqueness of the portfolio may prompt the hiring manager to ask you about it. You should simply state that it's a portfolio containing documentation of your qualifications and accomplishments. You might add something like, "It supports the claims I've made on my résumé, and I'll be using parts of it to help me prove to you that I'm the right person for this job."

The hiring manager may want to know more about where you got the portfolio and how it's put together, but be careful at this point not to get sidetracked. If the hiring manager wants to know more about how the **PoP Portfolio** was put together, say that you'll be happy to explain more about it at the end of the interview and that by the end of the interview the purpose of the **PoP Portfolio** will become clear.

At this point, your preparation for the interview will be very important! As we said, your clean résumé will be in the front pocket of your portfolio. If you've done your research, you'll have found a high-impact article about the industry, the company, or the individual with whom you're interviewing. This article should be in the front of the portfolio, so that **the hiring manager can't fail to notice the article you've copied and highlighted.** Even if neither of you mentions the article, its presence subtly shows the hiring manager that you have prepared well for the interview. He'll be pleased to see that you've documented your past performance and that you're serious about interviewing for the position. You'll immediately gain the respect of the hiring manager, who will know that you're not wasting his time—like many other candidates who come in unprepared or who treat the formal interview like an informational interview. It's very important that you take time to practice this introductory phase in advance, hopefully with someone who will role-play the interview with you. The more you practice this, the more confident you'll be.

Two Ways Not to Use Your Portfolio

There are two dangerous ways that we have seen people use a portfolio and at this point we believe it is worth a word of warning.

❖ Never take the portfolio out and show it page by page to a hiring manager. The purpose of the portfolio is to hold all your documentation, and in an interview you will only show what is appropriate for that specific interview.

❖ Do your best not to lose control of your portfolio. At times the interviewer may try to look ahead or take the portfolio and leaf through it. Try to tactfully avoid this.

The Interview Begins

Now the fun begins! During this part of the interview, you'll begin fielding questions. You'll have one distinct advantage over your competition if you've followed the steps above: you'll have already established credibility, so your answers will be better believed. This is very important in the interviewing process, because hiring managers are skeptical about the claims most candidates make about their pasts. That is why the **PoP Portfolio** is so important in the interviewing process.

As you respond to the hiring manager's questions, be sure to tell the stories of those experiences. A story is an entertaining and interesting way to show your strengths, and hiring managers like to hear them. The manager might say, "Tell me about your biggest accomplishment in your last job." This is a golden opportunity! Don't just say, "I received an Employee of the Month award a few times." *Tell the story* of how you did it and use the documentation you've prepared to illustrate your story. The impact will be terrific!

Don't Get "Lost"

"A number of career services professionals are reporting 'lost seniors,' students who are consciously choosing to forego the career center, on-campus recruitment, and other job-search activities in the mistaken belief that jobs are theirs for the asking, with little or no work required on their part."

- Job Outlook '99

The preparation you put into your **PoP Portfolio** will also help you to be more relaxed during the interviewing process, which will help you to listen better. Candidates who are very nervous often fail to focus on the content of the questions being asked. Their fear and panic cause them to ramble on and on in an effort to answer the question they thought they heard. You, on the other hand, will be at ease and can **practice good listening:** focus on what the other person is saying, rather than trying to frame your answer before he has finished the question.

Your PoP Portfolio and the preparation that you have put into it will help eliminate your fears better than anything else we have observed. Time and again, people we have trained to use the portfolio return to us and say, "I went from fearing the interview to actually enjoying it, once I got my documentation and company research in order!"

Identifying and Addressing Needs

One of the most important interviewing skills you'll need to develop is the ability to uncover and identify needs. A need could be anything, but most often it will be a job skill, experience, education, or a personal characteristic of the person who will best fill the position.

The first way to identify needs, of course, is through research and informational interviewing. At the appropriate time in the interview, you'll let the interviewer know you have researched the company, the industry, and the position that you are seeking. Share with them the needs you've identified and get agreement from them that those are definite needs for someone in this position. Specifically, you should have identified the top three needs of the position and prepared the documentation that will prove you can meet those needs as an employee. (*We recommend that you place copies of those pieces directly behind your résumé in the front pocket of your port-folio.)* But no matter how much advance work you do, there will still be some needs that will only be revealed at the interview.

Identifying Needs in the Interviewing Process

During the course of the interview, therefore, one of your main goals will be to identify the needs of the hiring manager. Keep your notepad open during the interview, and as you identify a need, jot it down, also making note of any documentation you have that will address that need. *(Make your notes quickly and unobtrusively; you don't want to keep your nose in your notebook the whole time!)* When you have the opportunity, you can respond by saying something like, "I heard you say that the person in this position needs to be such and such and I have documentation to prove that I can meet that need." Then show the hiring manager the relevant material in your portfolio.

Throughout the entire interview, **you should be listening for different clues that will help you identify the needs of the position,** as revealed by the hiring manager. Here are some questions that may help you uncover some of those needs:

❖ What are you looking for in the person you will be hiring for this position?

❖ What would the ideal background be for the person you hire for this position?

❖ What has made people whom you've hired in the past successful in this position?

❖ What would the perfect person for this job be like?

❖ What would I be doing in this position in a typical day or week?

❖ What has caused people to fail in this position in the past?

❖ Do you foresee any changes in the industry that may change this position in the near future?

One primary purpose of the interview, then, is for you to identify as many needs as you possibly can. Once you identify the needs, you can use the documentation in your **PoP Portfolio** to prove that you can meet those needs. At the end of the interview, you might want to leave copies of the most powerful documentation with the hiring manager.

Closing the Interview

The closing is the most important part of the interview, but **95% of people fail to close their interview effectively.** If you've been identifying needs, showing documentation, and telling stories that help prove to the hiring manager that you can meet those needs, then you are in a great position to close the interview. During the entire interview, you should be prioritizing, in your head or in your notes, which needs are the most important to the hiring manager. **Closing the interview is simply stating the principal needs that you've uncovered and briefly reminding the hiring manager how you meet those needs.** This should simply be a review of the things you have already discussed, and each point should be brief.

The final step, and one that many people never take, is to **ask for the job.** The reason to ask for the job or next interview is to get any objections out on the table. Candidates that do not ask never even find out why they didn't get offered the job or next interview. By asking for the job you get the opportunity to handle any objections a hiring manager may have.

Many people don't get the job simply by failing to ask for it! Remember the story of Bridget that we told in Chapter 2? At the end of her interview, she said, "I really want this job and I want to know what I have to do to get it." She made it clear that she wanted the job, and she effectively **put the ball back in the hiring manager's court!**

If the interview has shown you that this is the right job for you, then review how you meet their needs and simply ask, "Is there any reason why you can't offer me the position today?" And then just listen. What the hiring manager says next is very, very important. The responses will vary, but they'll fall into one of five general categories:

Getting the Job Offer

They offer you the position! At this point, you can **begin the process of negotiating the compensation package.** In some situations, there may be a set compensation package with little or no ability to negotiate. In other situations, the package is open to negotiation. (*Your informational interviews and research will be important in both situations. While you're doing your research and informational interviews, you'll want to do your best to determine your market value.*)

Taking the Next Step

The second response may be that they do not have the ability to offer you the job right now, but that there will be another round of interviews. **Your goal is to get invited back for that second interview,** so restate your original question, "Is there any reason why you can't invite me back for the next round of interviews?" If you're invited, great! If not, you need to overcome their objections as explained in the following section.

Pleasant Persistence

In many years of recruiting, we've heard lots of stories in which persistence pays off with a job offer. Here's one such story.

A few years ago, Roger S., Sales Manager of a Fortune 500 electronics company, was looking to hire a sales rep. He announced the opening in a want ad, asking for two years of experience selling electronic components. He got a ton of résumés in response, including one from Bill W., who did have two years of sales experience, but not in the electronics industry.

When Roger didn't respond to Bill's résumé, Bill called and requested an interview. Roger told Bill that he had received his résumé, but that he wanted to look at two other candidates who had more industry experience. Bill then asked if he could call back in a couple of weeks, just in case those other candidates didn't work out. Roger said that would be fine.

Bill wrote a follow-up letter, in which he thanked Roger for his time, and also reiterated why he would be a good candidate: he impressed upon Roger that he would do whatever it took to get into the electronics industry, because he knew his personality and high interest level would stand him in good stead.

Soon after, Roger was called out of town, so no hiring decision had been made when Bill called back in two weeks, as promised. Roger explained the delay and again kept Bill at bay, not inviting him in for an interview. Bill persisted, once again asking if he could call back in two weeks, in case the other candidates proved unsuitable. Roger agreed that it would be OK.

About a week later, Bill mailed Roger an interesting article that he had seen in a trade journal, attaching a note that said simply, "I thought you'd be interested in this. Bill W." Sure enough, about a week after that, Bill called to ask Roger if the position had been filled. It had not, and this time Roger invited Bill to come in for an interview. Eventually, Bill was hired, and he is now one of the top sales reps in that company!

In this case, the Proof of Performance was in Bill's persistence. Even though he was an underdog at the outset, Bill "outpersisted" his competition in a creative and pleasant manner.

Getting and Handling Objections

The interviewer may offer you a reason why you're not being offered the job or being invited back for a second interview. This presents you with a great opportunity! Implicit in the reason you're being given is a perception that you don't meet an important need. It's impossible to cover every need in an interview, and the hiring manager may simply have assumed that you can't meet a need. If you're able to demonstrate that you can indeed meet that need, you'll get a second chance at the job or an invitation to a second interview. If they don't give you a reason, of course you can't address it. **But if you're able to prove you can meet the need, you'll often be able to save the interview and get the offer.** Don't quit until they offer an objection you can't overcome.

Delay Response

The interviewer may tell you that they have many people to interview, and that they'll let you know when they make a decision. Your goal is to find out when the decision is going to be made and when you should follow up. The next step is to develop a persistent, but pleasant, strategy to follow-up. Start with a thank-you note. Then send a letter or fax with a piece of documentation that reinforces your qualifications for the position. You could also send an interesting article about the company or industry that expresses a need within the company, and then address how you meet that need.

No

Not being hired is indeed a letdown, but remember that a "No" only brings you one step closer to that ultimate "Yes!" No interview in which you've done a good job is ever wasted! There are several ways you can use a rejection to advance your job campaign, and your follow-up strategy will depend on the reason you weren't hired.

There are two basic reasons why you don't get hired: First, the interview may have revealed that you aren't completely qualified for the position—you simply can't overcome an objection. This will be disappointing if you really wanted the job, but **use it as an opportunity to learn what you must do in the future to get the job you want**. Take careful notes on why you weren't qualified, seek out the training and experience you lack, and then get documentation of your improved qualifications.

Letting Go

Being rejected for a job for which you appear to be well-qualified can be very frustrating. Use follow-up strategies to the make the most of an unsuccessful interview, but you should also learn to "let go" of the experience once the decision is out of your hands.

A well-known Hollywood producer/director once noted that in casting a film, he sees any number of qualified candidates—actors who could play a given role well. But eventually, it comes down to an intuitive decision about which people will work best together, about who will have that special chemistry that will make the movie compelling to watch. He compares casting to giving a dinner party, where you invite people that you think will get along well together, and sometimes not inviting good people who wouldn't be compatible.

It's much the same in any hiring situation. At some point, a hiring manager has to think how you would fit into the group you'd be working with and into the company culture. Eventually, they will have to consider intangibles.

But as our director friend says, "You should know that you put yourself out there very successfully. You should go to sleep that night, whether you got the job or not, saying 'I did that well. I performed well. And now it has nothing to do with me anymore; it's going to be because of others, because of combinations; it's going to be about the dinner party. And that I can't control. But, man, I can make this guy know that the next time he gives a dinner party, he ought to seriously consider me as a guest."

Give it your very best shot—and then let go of it!

At other times, you may appear to meet all the hiring criteria, yet you're not offered the job. This usually comes down to personality differences or other intangibles that you can't overcome. This will be frustrating, but you should realize that if the hiring manger is good at his job, **he *will* remember you and your strong presentation**. He may very well refer you to someone they know who has an opening that's exactly what you're looking for!

You can also ask for such a referral! We recommend that you should always ask for a referral, it's a discipline of good networking! Remember that the hiring manger is a well-networked professional, so don't be afraid to **ask for the names of individuals or professional organizations that could help you in your job search**. In these instances, an interview where you *don't* get the job may ultimately do you more good than if you'd gotten the offer!

Leaving the Interview

Once the interview is completed, shake hands with the hiring manager, thank him for his time, and review how you will be following up with him. When leaving the office, be sure to thank everyone who has helped you while you have been at the company for the interview. Remember that receptionists often give feedback to the hiring managers, so consider yourself "on stage" until you actually leave the company building.

Writing the Thank-You Note

Upon returning home, be sure to write a thank-you, even if you have been invited back for the second interview or even if you have been offered the position. The thank-you should be no longer than a one-page letter or card. In your letter or card, you should include these things:

❖ Thank the hiring manager for his time and for the interview.

❖ Briefly summarize the needs that were identified in the meeting and restate how you're able to meet the needs of the position.

❖ Briefly state the agreed-upon follow-up procedure in the final paragraph.

We suggest that you either e-mail or fax the text of your letter to the hiring manager the very next morning. You should also send him a hard copy of the letter. This assures that your name will be in front of the hiring manager at least twice in the next few days. If possible, include a copy of a new piece of documentation with your letter, as well.

In Conclusion

We wish you the very best in your career transition, whether you're just starting out or whether you're undertaking a career transition later in life. We're sure that your **Proof of Performance Portfolio** will be of inestimable value to you in this process, and that the activities involved in its preparation will give you the knowledge, the solid documentation, and the confidence you'll need to win the job you've dreamed of. But the process won't end once you're hired!

Your Proof of Performance Portfolio won't be just another book; it will become part of your life. It will be a total system approach ensuring that you'll be able to get the best jobs throughout your whole career and even if you decide to change to a new career. Your portfolio is really never complete. Continue to document your accomplishments, and keep track of the kinds of skills they represent.

In today's uncertain business climate, everyone needs to become an expert at the game of career transition. With your **PoP Portfolio** in hand, you're becoming a performance-based person, documenting your successes as you go. You'll know that you're prepared for whatever might happen and you'll realize that you have nothing to fear. You'll sleep soundly each night, confident that you'll have success at whatever you try.

Afterword

When to Move On: "Leaving the Mother Ship"

There I was, sitting in my beautiful office, working for a Fortune 100 privately-held company and making great money. The team of people I managed were like family — I loved them all. So why was I staring at the wall, feeling numb and not alive and exuberant, like I used to feel? Is that just the way it is when you get older? I hoped not!

My title was Corporate Recruiting Manager. My position offered me the opportunity to take several personality assessments for free, as companies tried to sell them to us. Looking over them, I noticed that several of these assessment tests said that I was in conflict in my job and that I wasn't using my creative talents to the degree that I should be. I was nagged by the question, "Is it time to move on?"

My mother was constantly telling me how lucky I was, and that I'd better never leave my job. She'd say, "You've finally become successful and you're building a great retirement fund. For God's sake, you get to fly around the country in the company's Lear jet with the company president whenever you want! What do you mean you're bored — are you crazy? I just don't get it!" I'd try to explain, "But Mom, I *am* bored. Just being comfortable isn't a major part of success for me. I have to feel challenged and have a passion for what I do."

One thing led to another, and after having a major talk with God, I quit. Needless to say, my mother went into shock! So did I, a little — it was like getting off an ocean liner and into a tiny rowboat out in the middle of the sea. There was no question that *fear* was trying to swamp me. But I kept on affirming that God was with me and was my guide in this new and exciting adventure. I told myself to enjoy this moment! As I looked back and saw the Mother Ship disappear over the horizon, I knew there was no turning back. I told myself, "Get rowing, Rick, a new island lies just ahead!"

Suddenly, it was like the doors of passion had opened up again. I shouted, "Wow! I'm alive, and I'm going for that career dream I wrote down almost ten years ago!" I was going to use my talents to create the soon-to-be *greatest career transition tool ever developed:* **The Proof of Performance Portfolio System** ™. It would help people during their career transition and its mission would be to "squash fear."

When I look back to how I felt during those last days on my old job and then think about how I feel today, there's no comparison! The risk paid off big time! Leaving my old career was a major turning point in my life and it all happened when the Lord and I teamed up and threw fear to the wind. Follow your passion and take God along!

Best wishes always,

Rick Nelles

About the Author:
Richard (Rick) Nelles

Rick Nelles is President of Career Directions, Inc., a recruiting firm specializing in the placement of sales professionals. For over 25 years he has been observing how the best candidates get the best jobs. He has seen the hiring process from every angle as owner of an executive search firm, as Sales Manager for a Fortune 500 company and as the Corporate Recruiting Manager for a Fortune 100 Privately Held company. His true stories will amaze and motivate you to become the best you can be in getting the job of your dreams.

Career Directions, Inc.

Career Directions, Inc. is a national recruiting service, and you're welcome to check out our website—www.career-directions.com—for job listings. You're welcome to contact us at any time with thoughts about how to improve the PoP Portfolio, or with stories from your own experience in the job market. If we publish your contribution in a future edition, you'll receive a free book from us!

We're also planning to publish a new book of inspirational stories of people going through career transition. We would love to hear your story, and if we publish it—you'll get recognition—you'll be a published author! Write us at Career Directions, Inc. or e-mail us at *cdi@career-directions.com*.

We Need and Want Your Help

As you discover new forms of documentation and new ideas for presenting that documentation in an interview, please be sure to share your ideas with us! Send a sample of the documentation and a brief story of how the documentation worked for you in the interview. Write us at Career Directions, Inc., 7525 Mitchell Rd, Suite 204, Eden Prairie, MN 55344 or e-mail your new ideas to **PoPstories@career-directions.com**. We'll post new ideas on our website at **www.career-directions.com**. If we use your idea in a future edition of this book, we'll send you a free copy. We look forward to hearing from you!

Career Transition Attitudes

The following page contains a chart relating to Career Transition Attitudes. We suggest that you remove the page and frame it and place it in a prominent place where you can daily remind yourself of the attitudes you need to display in order to become successful.

Positive Attitudes	Negative Attitudes
Optimistic	Pessimistic
Growing	Stagnant
Overcoming fear	Overcome by fear
Striving for excellence	Settling for mediocrity
Creative problem solver	Paralyzed by problems
A well developed written plan of attack to reach defined goals	No written plan of attack or defined goals
Planned & executed networking	Little or no networking
Enthusiasm	Indifference
Determined persistence	Quit when the going gets tough
Giving of oneself	Expecting things on a platter
Life happens for you	Life happens to you
"Make it happen" attitude	"See what happens" attitude
Involved	Isolated

Career Transition Attitudes

It's up to you to decide your attitude...

Elk River

May 29, 1999

To Whom It May Concern:

I am the Band Director at Elk River High School. Rick Nelles was a main ingredient in helping us to raise over $50,000 to go to New Orleans. His creative promotional skills sparked the whole band to sell the Portfolio Seminar. Rick is a real team motivator!

Sincerely,

Expanding Your Comfort Zone Worksheet

Activity to Work On: _____

Date Initiated	Goal Date	Action Step	Date Completed

Notes:

Proof of
Performance
Portfolio ™

Form #1

Proactive Documentation Planner

Accomplishment or Job Skill to Document

Goal Date

Forms of Documentation

- [ ] Reference Letter
- [ ] Testimonial Letter
- [ ] Story
- [ ] Work Evaluation
- [ ] Newspaper Article
- [ ] Certificate
- [ ] Award
- [ ] Prizes
- [ ] Published Article
- [ ] Diploma
- [ ] Test Results
- [ ] Picture
- [ ] Other:

Contacts

Contact 1	Work Phone	Home Phone
Position	Address	
Company		

Contact 2	Work Phone	Home Phone
Position	Address	
Company		

Completed and placed in PoP Portfolio on:

Placed in Section:

Proof of **Performance** Portfolio ™

Form #2

Proactive Career Goals

What I Want In My Career   **What I Don't Want In My Career**

Career Goals

Proactive Steps to Get the Job I Want In My Career

Inactive Steps That Lead to Career Boredom

(We've already completed this one for you!)

- No networking or informational interviews to find the best jobs.
- No written goals or plan to achieve your career dreams.
- An attitude of "just let it happen."
- Unwilling to take calculated risks.
- Quit when going gets tough.
- Lack of faith.
- Do not gather documentation.
- Do not build portfolio.

Proof of
Performance ™
Portfolio

Form #3

Work History

COMPANY		
ADDRESS		
CITY	STATE	ZIP
JOB TITLE	START DATE	END DATE
SUPERVISOR	START WAGE	END WAGE
REASON FOR LEAVING		
NOTES		

COMPANY		
ADDRESS		
CITY	STATE	ZIP
JOB TITLE	START DATE	END DATE
SUPERVISOR	START WAGE	END WAGE
REASON FOR LEAVING		
NOTES		

COMPANY		
ADDRESS		
CITY	STATE	ZIP
JOB TITLE	START DATE	END DATE
SUPERVISOR	START WAGE	END WAGE
REASON FOR LEAVING		
NOTES		

Proof of Performance
Portfolio™

Form #4

Network Planning Worksheet

Name	Company	Position
Home Phone	E-mail	Business Phone
Home Address	Business Address	
Home City, State & Zip	Business City, State & Zip	
Date of Initial Contact	Appointment Scheduled	Phone	In Person	AT

Information Summary

☐ Career Information ☐ Industry Information ☐ Company Information ☐ Competitor Information ☐ Customer Information

Referrals

Referral	Company	Position
Home Phone	Business Phone	Address
Referral	Company	Position
Home Phone	Business Phone	Address
Referral	Company	Position
Home Phone	Business Phone	Address

Proof of
Performance
Portfolio ™

Form #5

Needs Worksheet

Company	Appointment
Address	Interviewer
	Position

Needs Identified

Need Identified	Source	How I meet the need	Documentation

Notes:

Proof of
Performance
Portfolio™

Form #6

I DREAM AND START TO BELIEVE IN A NEW EXCITING GOAL

COURAGE STARTS TO BUILD AND GETS STRONGER

I GET MORE COMMITTED TO A GOAL

ACTION PROCESS STARTS

ROAD BLOCKS AND HURDLES COME UP

FEAR AND DOUBT CREEP IN

WHAT IF I FAIL?

DECISION TIME!

ROAD TO SUCCESS	ROAD TO BOREDOM
▪ ATTITUDE—I DON'T QUIT—EVER!!	▪ ATTITUDE—MAYBE THIS ISN'T FOR ME
▪ I FOCUS, RE-VISUALIZE DREAM, LOOK AT PICTURE GOALS	▪ I START TO LOOK FOR SOMETHING ELSE
▪ I KEEP THE ACTION PROCESS GOING	▪ I LOSE DISCIPLINE TO ACT
▪ I READ, WORK OUT, LISTEN TO MOTIVATIONAL TAPES	▪ I PROCRASTINATE—STAY UNMOTIVATED
▪ MY PERSISTENCE GETS ME TO GOAL	▪ I MISS ANOTHER OPPORTUNITY—NOTHING HAPPENS
▪ I WIN!!! LIFE IS GOOD!	▪ I AM BORED—UNHAPPY

Career Transition Attitudes & Actions

It's up to you to decide your attitudes and actions. . .

Winning Attitudes & Actions	Losing Attitudes & Actions
POSITIVE A "LIFE IS EXCITING" ATTITUDE	NEGATIVE A WHINY "POOR ME" ATTITUDE
HARD WORKING	LAZY
ACUTELY AWAKE/AWARE	ASLEEP AT THE WHEEL
FAITH	LACK OF FAITH
CREATIVE PROBLEM SOLVER	PARALYZED BY PROBLEMS
WELL DEVELOPED WRITTEN PLAN OF ATTACK TO REACH DEFINED GOALS	NO WRITTEN PLAN OF ATTACK OR DEFINED GOALS
PLANNED & EXECUTED NETWORKING	LITTLE OR NO NETWORKING
LOOKING SHARP	POOR APPEARANCE
DETERMINED PERSISTENCE	QUIT WHEN THE GOING GETS TOUGH
EXERCISING TO STAY HEALTHY	SITTING ON A COUCH WATCHING TV
FEELING GOOD ABOUT YOURSELF	LOW SELF-ESTEEM
"I WILL MAKE IT HAPPEN" ATTITUDE	"SEE WHAT HAPPENS" ATTITUDE
DEVELOPING A PROOF OF PERFORMANCE PORTFOLIO	DEPENDING ON JUST A RESUME

IT'S YOUR CHOICE

Index

The Click and Easy™ Online
Career Resource Centers –

Books, videos, software, training materials, articles, and advice for job seekers, employers, HR professionals, schools, and libraries

Visit us online for all your career needs:

www.impactpublications.com
(career superstore and Impact Publications)

www.winningthejob.com
(articles and advice)

www.contentforcareers.com
(syndicated career content for job seekers, employees, and Intranets)

www.veteransworld.com

www.greentogray.com

www.bluetogray.com
(military transition databases and content)